DISPLAY

DISPLAY

LAURENCE LLEWELYN-BOWEN

DISPLAY

USING EVERYDAY OBJECTS TO CREATE GREAT INTERIORS

Stylist Helen Carey

COLLINS & BROWN

CONTENTS

First published in Great Britain in 2000 by
Collins & Brown Limited
London House
Great Eastern Wharf
Parkgate Road
London SW11 4NQ

Distributed in the United States
and Canada by
Sterling Publishing Co.
387 Park Avenue South
New York, NY 10016, USA

9 8 7 6 5 4 3 2 1

British Library Cataloguing-in-Publication Data: A catalogue
record for this book is available from the British Library.

ISBN: 1-85585-798-7

Editor: Michelle Pickering
Design: Yelaggab
Main photography: Tino Tedaldi
Photography on pages 1 and 7: Nicky Johnston
Stylist: Helen Carey
Assistant stylist: Pia Munden
Indexer: Dorothy Frame

Manufactured in Singapore by Classic Scan Pte Ltd
Printed in China by Dai Nippon

This book was typeset using Frutiger and Walbaum.

CANDLES: Burning candles can be a fire hazard. Take care at
all times that candles are firmly secured and that lighted
candles are never left unattended.

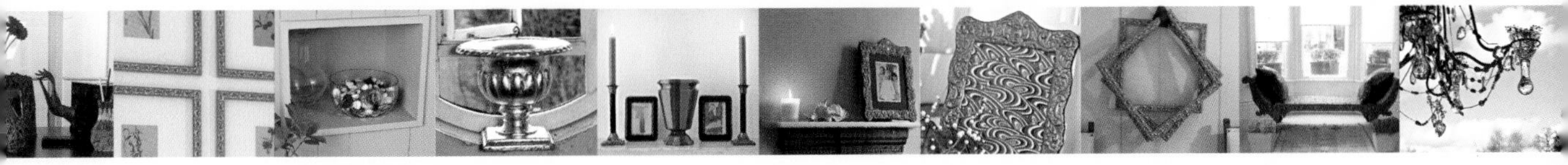

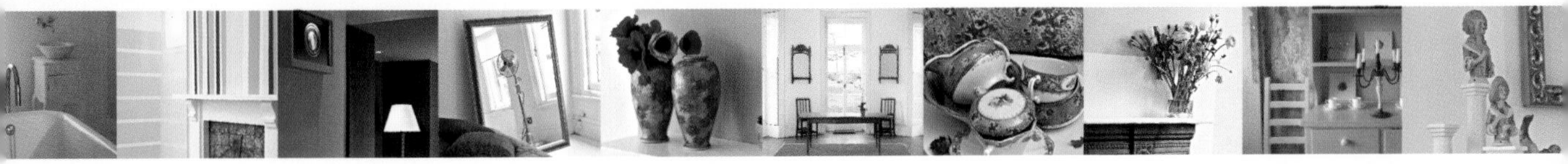

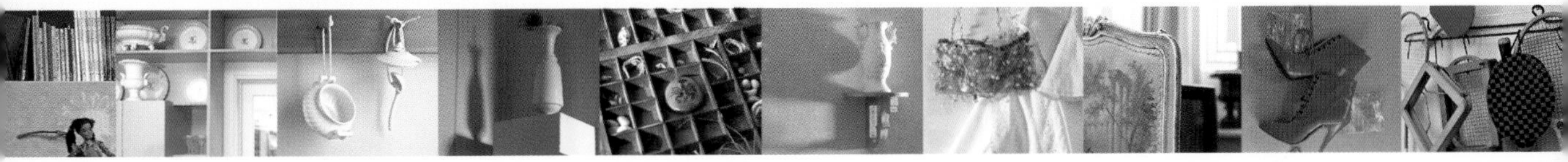

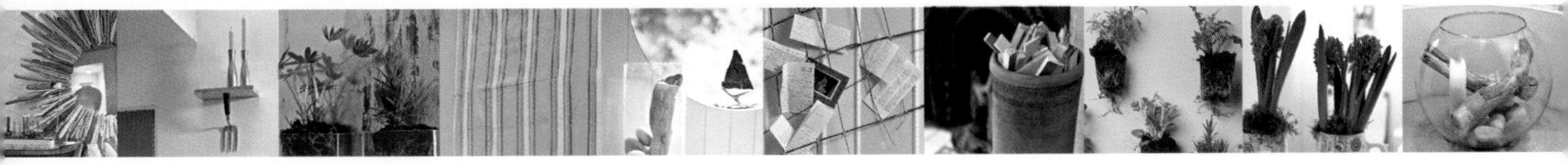

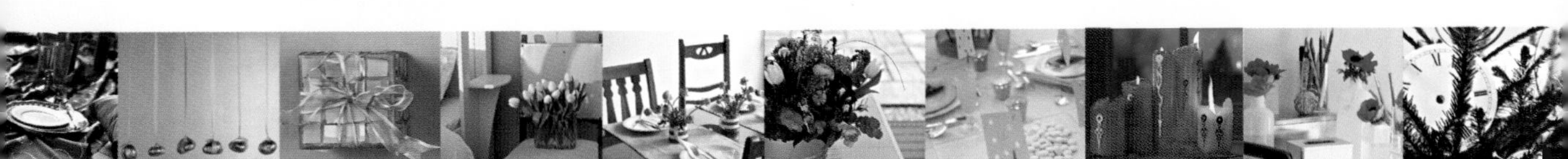

foreword

Late 20th-century living was a very simplistic affair. Many of us strove to create surroundings in which one or two carefully chosen, beautiful objects provided the only decorative details. It is interesting to note that every other period in history has held the opposite view – rooms were decorated with a riot of detail, with objects stacked in serried ranks and every whatnot supporting a whatsit. More recently, though, clutter has become one of the sternest swear words in our collective aesthetic vocabulary. However, a home with neither clutter nor mess is rarely achievable in the real world of modern living. Even if you're blessed with a tidy streak, the constraints of children, pets, partners and, above all, lack of time can make a tidy home impossible to achieve and lead to a world of unsuccessful interiors lived in by unhappy people.

This book is here to help you work within the realistic parameters of the modern home. There is little point recommending a white shag-pile carpet if you have a hairy black dog that is going to shed its hairs in all the wrong places, or praising an archly minimal bathroom if you always take at least five bottles into the shower. The key to remember is that all objects have a beauty. Sometimes that beauty may only be in the eye of its owner, but the point is that there is always a way to turn even the humblest collection of objects into a gorgeous still life – in essence, to display your possessions in such a way that they will help to create an attractive but practical home that you will enjoy living in. Interior design has to be practical for each individual and, though storage can rid the intensely banal from view, I have always found that surrounding ourselves with objects that have a specific association – a history to them or an aesthetic value – gives interiors that crucial feeling of comfort and personality.

There is a temptation with this kind of book to use only stylish elements and say 'right, that's three beautiful vases in a row'. However, as a father, a dog owner and a busy human being, I know that this is only half the story. I have set out to illustrate this book with the kind of clutter that we all possess. I've also set out to address issues such as technology in interiors, generation gaps and sports equipment with the same eye for composition one might use for arranging the poshest of knick-knacks in a world-renowned museum. The guidelines are simple and accessible, but the basic message is clear: create order out of chaos and give emphasis to elements you adore, leaving less glamorous objects to the shadows.

introduction

The home is one of the few corners of our lives that we can arrange entirely on our own terms. What we wear, what we say and what we do will inevitably be considered, appraised and judged in a public context at some point or other. Our interiors, however, are private. We can invite the outside world in if we so choose but, ultimately, other people's reactions to the way in which we arrange our personal worlds are irrelevant. We decorate our homes according to our own tastes and for our own pleasure.

Having said that, there are inevitably constraints on what we can achieve: the practical constraints set by the needs of others sharing our space; the economic constraints of working within a budget; and the constraints that spring from a lack or surfeit of space. In addition, the realities of busy modern living can also restrict what we do with our homes, since few of us have the time to create or look after a high-maintenance or overly contrived interior design. However, none of these constraints is insurmountable.

SHOEBOX STORAGE Decorated shoeboxes provide attractive free storage for those items that you just cannot bear to display.

If you have small children to accommodate within your design scheme, turn to Generation Game on pages 68–95 to discover ways to minimize and even utilize the plethora of objects that having children necessitates. Even those working within the tightest of budgets can realize their design dreams – Outside In on pages 96–125 shows how you can use the cheapest of raw materials to create stunning displays. Upscale Downscale on pages 40–67 looks at the problems of scale, both of the architectural environment and of the objects displayed within. As far as high

THE ART OF DISPLAY This book looks at the various display dilemmas from a multitude of angles (below, left to right): how to create both formal and informal arrangements; playing with scale and dimensions; encompassing the everyday objects of family life into the home successfully; bringing the outside into the interior to create natural displays; and producing festive arrangements that delight the senses.

maintenance is concerned, turn to Formal Informal on pages 14–39 to discover ways in which you can create the ambience you want in your home while keeping it practical and easy to maintain. Then, of course, there's Movable Feasts on pages 126–155. This is where you can indulge your festive spirit to create an environment full of pleasurable but stylish delights.

The two essentials for achieving successful displays are: playing around (trial and error make the planet revolve) and confidence. The first is what wet weekends are made for, and the second is why mankind invented a procedure for transmuting the grape into wine. In the meantime, on the following pages you will find a few tips to get you started.

EXPERIMENT WITH CONFIDENCE The best way to achieve a successful display is by trial and error. Don't be afraid to move things around until you achieve a pleasing result.

PERSONAL TASTE

There is no such thing as good or bad taste. It is you who must decide whether you like or dislike the way you have decorated a room. Is it close to the vision you had formed in your mind before you started? Is it an eloquent expression of you? Does it really answer your needs? These questions may not be easy to answer but they are necessary if you are to create a home environment in which you can be happy.

FINISHING TOUCHES

The finishing touches can make or break a scheme. In fact, there is really no such thing as minimalism: even a completely empty room will have a light switch, and the position, style and finish of that switch will make a visual statement. In reality, most of us like to steer a course between the excesses of chilly modernism and the frantic blowziness of traditional clutter, but only you can decide how close to one or the other you wish to steer.

CHOICE OF OBJECTS

The majority of the objects that we have at our design disposal will be things we have bought specially to bring a particular scheme to life. There is, however, another class of object that needs to be incorporated but over which we have minimal aesthetic control: the inherited, the sentimental, the useful; all of those essential bits and pieces for which we have to find a home. The trick is to blend them all together without compromising any of the objects themselves or the rooms in which they are displayed.

CREATING CONTEXTS

To create a successful display that makes a visual statement while harmonizing with the rest of the room, it is necessary to place objects within some kind of suitable context. Appraise each object with a fresh eye, unprejudiced by perceived notions. Look hard; everything has something going for it somewhere. Often a change of context can reincarnate an object that has been long discarded.

CREATING LINKS

There will always be times when you need to go out and find an object that will link an arrangement and make the whole thing spring to life. Look for connections in colour, pattern, shape or form; the link does not have to be exact but simply suggestive of the other items in the display. The new object could be something beautiful in its own right or something more pedestrian that would go unnoticed on its own but that will bring the perfect tone to the right display.

ACHIEVING BALANCE

The key to a successful arrangement is usually balance, which can easily be achieved by creating a symmetrical display. If you don't have pairs of objects, however, remember that everything has a visual 'weight'. A tall glass vase is light and airy; a dark bronze bust is weighty and ponderous. If you want to place the bust at one end of a mantelshelf and balance it with a vase at the other, you will need to add a few heavy objects to the vase end to create equilibrium – a few dark, shiny pebbles, for example.

style labs | an explanation

Each chapter contains one or two 'style labs'. These special feature pages are intended to give a quick illustration of the main display points under discussion in that particular chapter by showing the same object or type of object in four different contexts to help you visualize the solution in your own interior. One of the problems with trying to find usable solutions for today's interiors is the sheer diversity of decorating styles. The fact that we have all become such aesthetic individualists is worthy of heartfelt applause, but many people find it difficult to see past the surface style to the fundamental design points that are being applied.

With this in mind, four different categories that express the key approaches to decorating in the 21st century have been chosen: ultra contemporary, romantic, rich and soft modern. Although this inevitably results in generalizations, it does help to illustrate how objects can be displayed successfully to suit a variety of styles and tastes, as well as emphasizing the design solution under discussion. In reality, of course, most of us favour a combination of design styles, and we will pick and choose to suit our own personalities and individual tastes.

◁ ULTRA CONTEMPORARY

This is all about hard-edged, uncompromising, 'see it as it is' design. Anyone who has tried this design discipline knows just how contrived and correct you have to be to achieve efficient simplicity. It is a master class and needs design nerves of steel.

▷ ROMANTIC

Pretty much anything goes in the romantic camp. So much of what surrounds the romantic tells a story, either from its own history or from a history it would like to be part of. Simple objects can sit quite easily next to more *recherché* elements in an eclectic mix of sentiment and design.

◁ RICH

If romantic design is a gentle kiss on the cheek, rich design is a fully fledged embrace. It is about making a bold, flavourful statement that denotes an outgoing, perhaps slightly escapist personality. Although rich decorating needs detail and luxury, which normally come at a price, with a little ingenuity even everyday objects can become dramatic focal points.

▷ SOFT MODERN

This is perhaps the most popular style category. It is all about not subscribing to extremes but instead choosing elements from many different styles. It allows you to create an interior that reflects contemporary lifestyles, while still retaining some traditional elements. It is a very personal style that can evolve with you and your home, and that remains largely unconstrained by rules.

Few people today live 'formal' lives – we are too busy for the high-maintenance etiquette that formality requires. As a result, we often find ourselves with objects, acquired by inheritance or perhaps as wedding gifts, that were designed to fulfil functions associated with a long dead, formal past that is irrelevant to modern living. However, these objects can be made to suit today's informal lifestyles and become a welcome part of our interiors. Inevitably, though, there are those who swing the other way – for whom a bit of grandeur, a sniff of days gone by, is a longed for accent in an otherwise 'now' interior. For both factions there is hope. Perhaps the most basic choice to be made when displaying objects in a formal or informal manner is to decide whether to

formal | informal

arrange them symmetrically or asymmetrically. Human beings are physically symmetrical. Having the same elements on both sides, of the same dimensions and at the same angles, was a prerequisite in the ancient Greeks' canon of beauty. That recipe for gorgeousness still haunts us today and casts a long, perfectly balanced shadow over many of our aesthetic decisions within the home. Symmetry is largely instinctive and is therefore the easiest way to create a formal display, which is why in the antiques world a pair of objects will always command a greater price than two single ones. It is impossible to make a symmetrical arrangement feel informal but, oddly, an asymmetrical display can achieve either formality or informality, provided a few rules are observed.

symmetry | symmetry

There is a persuasive argument to be made that all design is based on the proportions of the human body. Classical architecture derived its sense of proportion and its commitment to symmetry from the human body. It is perhaps because of this relationship to our own physical features that we instinctively find ourselves drawn to symmetrical arrangements – they feel natural and uncontrived to us. Of course, in reality true symmetry never occurs in nature, so in a way imposing symmetry on our lives is like the imposition of human order over natural chaos.

Symmetry is about the straightforward balance of objects – if an imaginary line ran down the centre of a symmetrical arrangement, each side would be an exact mirror image of the other. When we think of classical elegance, our vision is almost always symmetrical. A symmetrically arranged group of objects is one of the most formal interior statements that you can make and, as a result, carries with it connotations of control and sophistication. Until the 20th century, objects were deliberately manufactured in pairs or multiples of pairs in order to make symmetrical arrangements easy to achieve.

The pursuit of symmetry requires a space that is itself symmetrical, with no nooks or crannies to upset the equilibrium. Although fireplaces are sometimes off-centre in a room, they are rarely asymmetrical and therefore provide the ideal display place for paired objects.

The human brain is a very literal organic computer that will try to establish an order or pattern in anything it sees. As a result, if you arrange objects in even numbers, your mind will instantly start pairing things together. Symmetrical decorating is, in essence, seeking to achieve restful, disciplined, rhythmic order that celebrates how clever we humans are to have stepped outside the untidy asymmetry of Mother Nature.

SYMMETRICAL OCCASIONAL TABLE Although it uses contemporary objects, this table arrangement is a direct reflection of the contrived, symmetrical groupings of the 17th and 18th centuries. Two chairs have been paired either side of the table, on which two lamps reflect each other and a clock and a picture mark the invisible centre line. The arrangement works because the objects have colour or finish in common.

SYMMETRICAL PICTURE FRAMES

It is difficult to imagine anything more pleasing than the regular rhythm created by symmetrically hung pictures. Here, four pictures in identical frames, hung with a consistent space around each image, create a larger statement. Hanging the pictures in a row would draw attention to the constituent parts and shatter the illusion of a large scale. Interestingly, because the pictures themselves have a romantic feel, it seemed inappropriate to arrange the china objects on the mantelshelf in a symmetrical and therefore intellectual way. The head has here lost to the heart.

NEGATIVE/POSITIVE TABLESCAPE The dividing line in this symmetrical arrangement is no longer invisible but sharply stated by the contrasting colours of the paired tables. However, the symmetry of the group could have been lost if it were not for the runner linking them. The colour and tone of the objects have been chosen to create contrast and produce a negative/positive display.

f o r m a l | i n f o r m a l

SYMMETRICAL WINDOW BAY Although this is a contemporary photograph of a modern interior, this image illustrates the timeless tradition of symmetrical arrangement. The ornate day bed in the window bay makes a tranquil horizontal line that is gently softened by the elegantly carved curves of the day bed and the plush soft leather cushions. Stone planters densely filled with tiny-leaved houseplants make a softly formal statement that balances the arrangement and removes any over-rigorous corners that might make this grouping uncomfortable on the eye.

asymmetry |

Modernist architects of the 20th century such as Le Corbusier purposely set out to shatter the inherited constraints of symmetrical classicism. This deliberate effort to shock the eye away from balance was greeted as a decisive break towards a new modern style. Asymmetrical arrangements fall into two categories: the unbalanced but nevertheless carefully weighted exercises of Le Corbusier; and the random, organic arrangement of objects inspired by the untidiness of nature.

Asymmetrical arrangements demand far more thought and skill than placing objects symmetrically either side of an imaginary centre line. It is a bizarre fact that to make a pile of books look uncontrived takes far more contrivance than stacking them in symmetrical rows. This is because the logical human mind always tries to create order out of chaos and, as a result, the messages the eye sends to the brain are analyzed and an intellectual process tries to pair objects together.

If you feel like a child of nature, you could simply scatter objects on a surface and leave them there, although relying on a random factor for your interior decoration needs faith. Modern asymmetry, however, needs thought. The finished effect should be as balanced as a symmetrical arrangement, so, if you imagine an invisible set of scales, the objects on the right should have the same visual weight as those on the left. Weight is calculated by considerations such as height, width and density of colour. Another way of looking at it is to move the fulcrum of the weighing scales off-centre. If your centre line moves to the left – dividing the objects into a third and two-thirds – the objects on the narrower left side need to be heavier (that is to say, more dominant) than the lighter objects on the wider right side. Clever stuff, and it works.

ASYMMETRICAL PICTURE FRAMES
If a single picture frame had been hung directly on the centre line between the two chairs, a rather chilly classical effect would have been the result. Instead, three frames hung at different angles deliberately subvert the balance of the mirror image of the chairs to produce an informal statement.

ORGANIC TABLESCAPE On the tabletop above everything has been placed to create a natural, uncontrived effect, and guess what? It took ages. For this kind of informality, instinct has to take over; if you think too hard, the effect will be lost. The objects have been selected to reflect each other in colour and mood, and then great pains taken to make the arrangement look casual rather than formal.

ASYMMETRICAL OCCASIONAL TABLE

Here, the symmetrical occasional table display from page 16 has been rearranged to create an asymmetrical display. Only a single lamp and chair have been used, instead of the matching pairs, but a sisal wastepaper basket has been added to achieve a perfectly balanced arrangement of modern asymmetry. If the tabletop were a seesaw, the fulcrum would be more or less halfway through the clock. The vertical weight of the lamp, the clock and the wastebasket on the left is equal to that of the dark, heavy chair and the picture on the right. This system of visual weight was much used by classical painters, who would make sure that the heavy, dark, left-hand third of their landscape painting balanced the lighter, larger area of the remaining two-thirds on the right-hand side.

ASYMMETRICAL WINDOW BAY The constituent parts of the symmetrical arrangement on page 19 are present here but arranged asymmetrically. By rejigging the composition and deliberately overweighting the left-hand side, an informal effect has been achieved. By building an element of disorder into the arrangement, it will take a lot of empty coffee cups and discarded newspapers to make this room look untidy – unlike rigidly symmetrical schemes, which scream high maintenance.

playing up | emphasizing

For anyone lucky enough to live in a grand, lofty space, there is often a problem getting more workaday contemporary objects to live up to their surroundings. These days, with so much importance placed on reducing costs and swiftness of manufacture, it is difficult to find objects that match the generous proportions or rich effect of antiques.

WINDOW AND URN

If you are the proud owner of an unusual architectural detail, such as this *'oeil de boeuf'* round window, you can show it off by drawing attention to it. The neoclassical architects of the late 18th and early 19th centuries often put stone urns in round niches, and it is that look that has inspired this arrangement. The object in the window may be a plastic urn rather than a grand stone one, but a lustrous embellishment of fake gold leaf gives it a borrowed grandeur.

Throughout the 20th century, living spaces seemed to contract mercilessly, leaving us to look around our rooms and feel that our personalities were potentially far larger than the spaces they inhabited. Most people dream of finding themselves in the enviable position of having to live up to their surroundings. If you find yourself in such a situation but cannot afford to buy expensive luxury items, don't worry as there is a lot you can do to make humdrum objects look more special. The first step is to find the right context and to decide on one object that is going to make the required statement. Too much clutter and the message is likely to be diffused, not only because you will not be able to see the wood for the trees but also because you will risk overstraining your budget. Don't overlook the obvious – you may well have something already in place that is halfway there but, because of overfamiliarity, seems not quite man enough for the job.

The next step is to maximize the effect, and to do this you will need to restrain quite severely any innate sense of subtlety you may have. In order to catch the eye and conjure up that 'wow' factor, it is almost impossible to go too far over the top as long as you make sure that whatever you do is as well executed as possible. In addition to filling a gap in your decorating scheme, playing up an object is immensely satisfying because you will achieve an entirely personal, unique statement that no one else could ever possess.

WINDOW AND CHANDELIER The finished effect of grandeur in this room belies the humble origins of the chain-store chandelier, which has been embellished with glass beads. By placing the chandelier in front of the window, the glass beads are shown to their best advantage in both daylight and candlelight. Crystal, glass or even plastic drops from junk shop chandeliers cost very little and can be reassembled in a baroque fashion on the substructure of a basic metal chandelier fitting using fine wire.

GOLDEN URN Putting a plastic urn in its nude, down-market state on a lovely old stone balustrade (below) or in a lavish interior (right) would please no one. To match the richness of the setting, the urn needs to achieve the same weight of luxury. If the urn is to live outside, real gold leaf must be used, as the elements will not tarnish it. This might sound extravagant, but the combined cost of urn and gold will come to less than the same urn in cast concrete.

CHANDELIER The grand interior pictured on the left shows how just a few well-chosen objects can produce an incredibly rich effect, which can be maximized by replacing an ordinary pendant light with an elaborate chandelier. If you are lucky enough to have plaster cornicing or a ceiling rose, you can make the chandelier seem even more luxurious by painting the plaster to match the finish of the light fitting (below). This is a perfect way of drawing the eye upwards.

playing down | minimizing

CRYSTAL BOWL A cut-crystal bowl might catch the light but in today's interiors it screams 1970s suburban chic. The key to displaying such a piece successfully is to try to draw the eye away from the object's offending elements. The solution used here was to fill the crystal bowl with polished pebbles that had been collected on family walks along the beach. The pebbles help to give the formal punchbowl a more earthy aura and take the edge off the ornate cuts in the crystal. This display also has the advantage that you can add to the collection whenever more pocketfuls of pebbles find their way home.

SILVER FRAME Ornate silver frames holding engagement photographs, formal christening line-ups or dreamy bridal pictures, placed on top of a glossy piano or sideboard, are a decidedly middle-class cliché. Silver frames are gorgeous objects in their own right but are often compromised by the photographs they contain. Frames should be used to emphasize and draw attention to two-dimensional images but there is no reason you cannot frame a less usual item, such as the beautiful wrapping paper displayed here.

SILVER CUTLERY Rather than being relegated to its velvet-lined canteen, this silver cutlery has achieved a new, informal incarnation by being displayed, ready for use, in rough terracotta pots. This sends a clear and comforting message: you are going to display your luxurious gift proudly but you will bend it to suit your decorating scheme rather than allowing it to dominate.

Most of us possess a few things that we would not choose to buy ourselves, but that have emotional or sentimental importance in our lives. Certainly, most married couples have a wedding present or two – lurking in a cupboard like a mad relative bricked up in the east wing – that makes a discordant, 'traditional' noise in their otherwise modern lives. However, with a little cunning, you can bring out the charm and relevance in most objects.

Wedding presents or inherited items are often intimidating because they are of far higher value than the objects we can afford to buy for ourselves. A shelf with a hugely expensive silver photograph frame displayed next to two plywood frames from the local thrift store can simply serve to highlight the relative cheapness of most of our belongings. However, there is no need to hide the offending piece of silver, as there are a few simple things you can do to make such seemingly disparate objects blend together well. For example, play up the wooden frames by embellishing them with silver leaf and use them to display a couple of beautiful postcards, and play down the glittery ornate frame by utilizing it to display a piece of pretty wrapping paper. This way, you can take pleasure in the handful of luxury items that you possess without your less glamorous belongings becoming overwhelmed by them.

style lab | fireplaces

Before central heating the fireplace was the only source of heat in a room, so it inevitably became the focal point. The fireplace and, more importantly, the mantel above it are universally relied upon to make the big statement that sums up the decorative style of the room. The natural urge is to go for symmetry but there are alternatives.

PLAYING DOWN
The mantelshelf of this plain, almost rustic bedroom fireplace has been simply furnished with a scented candle and a cluster of shells. At first glance, the ornate silver frame alongside these simple objects might seem inappropriate but, because the picture within the frame is so delightfully informal, any pomposity has been subverted.

PLAYING UP Cool, modern interiors often lack a 'wow' factor. Here, a contemporary photographic print grabs the attention because, although it is a simple depiction of a single flower, its monumental scale forces you to catch your breath. Immediately, the rather ordinary fireplace feels more imposing but without compromising the modernity of the scheme.

SYMMETRY This traditional arrangement owes an emphatic nod in the direction of the Georgians. Its serenity is due to the gentle U shape created by an imaginary line running from the top of the left-hand candle down to the lip of the wooden urn and rising gracefully again to the top of the candle on the right. If the candlesticks had been placed directly next to the urn, the profile of the grouping would be a more staccato zigzag shape, less likely to induce restfulness.

ASYMMETRY This softly modern fire surround has been given a suitably contemporary arrangement, with natural elements such as pebbles and dried grasses helping to balance the asymmetry of the mantel display. The eye-catching blue of the square plates is visually very heavy, so it needs quite a few of the lighter objects – the square glass vases of long grasses and pebbles – to stop the finished effect from becoming unbalanced.

To sit happily together in the same space, objects need to have something in common. Putting particular items together because they share a function, or have a link because they are all used for the same specific activity, accounts for most of the arrangements that surround us. In the same way, obvious similarities in colour or material make for instant collections. However, infinitely more subtle effects can be achieved with a display of diverse objects if they share an intellectual or emotional link.

A purely decorative arrangement of disparate objects needs to be united by a shared theme. Grouping objects with an overall colour scheme is one method of doing this and, in many ways, is an easy step in the right direction. Grouping items that have a relationship based on their origins, either geographically or historically, sounds far more complicated to achieve but in fact does not have to be so cut and dried.

The organic, curvaceous lines of the exotic East were unknown in the rigorously classical canon of Western design until trade opened with the Far East in the late 16th century, when the straight lines of the Renaissance were dramatically subverted by Japanese artefacts hitting the European trade markets. Oriental design has since enjoyed a lengthy influence on Western taste, and the high baroque of the 17th century, rococo of the 18th, and baroque and rococo revivals of the 19th century all drew their inspiration from Japanese and Chinese styles. With this in mind, truly Oriental objects taken straight from their Eastern context can work very well with European and American pieces that have taken the East as their inspiration but gone on to establish their own specific flavour.

As well as using geographical origins to establish a bond, there are other types of provenance that you could explore, such as items from the sea, objects culled from woodlands, or bits and pieces taken from metropolitan living.

KITCHEN SHELVES Open kitchen shelves need not be a chaotic jumble where practical constraints override design. Instead, celebrate the fact that everything in the kitchen has been produced with the same goal in mind – filling your stomach. Make full use of the colourful packaging of foodstuffs but punctuate these items with cooler shelves of neutral objects such as glassware, on which the eye can rest.

ORIENTAL TABLE DISPLAY The link between the objects on this Javanese-style table is obviously the Orient. The small bronze mirror frame is a modern cast of a Victorian baroque original but its silhouette has a decidedly Eastern flavour. The fluid organic arrangement itself makes a firm nod in the direction of Oriental asymmetry, and texture plays a strong role, with the rough surface of the woven balls complementing the flaky verdigris finish of the Oriental hand on a base.

colour | compatibility

The mind is like a worried sheep dog, anxiously surveying a collection of objects to find lost sheep and reunite them with the flock. In display terms, therefore, the brain is least taxed and most easily satisfied when the eye sees a group of identically coloured objects. It will forgive a jagged outline or a slightly off-centre composition for the sheer joy of not having to work too hard to take in the arrangement. Take care, though, that your eye-catching one-colour arrangement does not dominate the interior.

BLUE EARTHENWARE This charming rustic-blue earthenware presents a romantic, higgledy-piggledy display on a country-style windowsill. You feel confident that this collection has happened over a number of years via a series of junk shop trawls.

As a starting point, let's be frank about one-colour arrangements: they have to be carefully balanced or they overstep the mark and become too dominant. A vista of Georgian blue glass on a mantelshelf — tall vase in the middle flanked by paired candlesticks, a brace of rose bowls and identical spill pots — may be the height of coordinated formality but it is almost so perfect it hurts. Instead, a rambling display of mismatched shapes in the same hue makes for a much more informal, far more relaxing display statement.

For most of us, a one-colour collection is an organic affair that revolves around disparate objects bought at different times or coming from a variety of sources. The collection has a lovely, open-ended feel that never finishes — around every corner there is the potential to find a new member for the club. As well as using a mix-and-match approach, another way to subvert the inbuilt formality of a one-colour arrangement is to play on the differences in texture. An all-white display could include glossy porcelain, rough natural textures such as shells, and matt white objects that have a smooth, stony feel.

GREEN VASES The jade green of these three vases links them instantly, although the vase used for the lamp base is 17th-century Oriental and the flanking pair are 20th-century European. However, it is the fact that each vase is different that brings the arrangement to life.

The behaviour of light, which is either reflected or absorbed by different surfaces, can provide an added dimension to the arrangement that will continue to change and delight as the light alters throughout the day. Differences in scale can help, too. Having an arrangement of objects of identical height and colour will make a very dense display. While this can be used for dramatic effect, varying the outline of the arrangement makes a statement that many would find easier to live with.

ALL-WHITE CERAMICS The whiteness of the objects is the obvious link in this ceramic display. Although potentially dull, the arrangement gets its visual excitement from the differences between the surface textures of the various items.

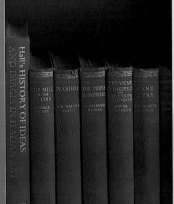

COLOUR-CODED BOOKSHELVES

Arranging books by author or subject can be death to decent display. Instead, try organizing books according to height and colour. The key to arranging objects is to create rhythms, and colour is the perfect way of doing this. Here, orange, black, neutral, burgundy and yellow book spines have been grouped together in rows, creating a pleasing display rather than a jumble of wildly contrasting colours. The vertical book spines allow the eye to move gently over the bookshelves but, if you have books of greatly varying heights, you can overcome this problem by stacking the smaller ones horizontally until they reach the same height as the taller upright spines. Sets of old or antique books can be used as attractive highlights along the shelves, as can pieces of china, which act as unexpected objects for the eye to rest upon at intervals.

Playing with scale – that is, making small things appear more prominent and forcing large elements to fade into the background – is an important part of interior design. One of the trickiest projects to tackle is how to display small objects within a large setting, without them losing their impact. Even trickier, however, is getting large elements to work in a restricted area without them becoming too dominant. Achieving success will take a degree of thought and a lot of trial and error. When successful, however, it is possible to create sophisticated displays that make a room more than worthy of being featured on the cover of a glossy interiors magazine. This chapter provides some basic ideas on how rooms themselves – the architectural frameworks for your

upscale | downscale

displays – can be 'upscaled' or 'downscaled', as well as looks at the various ways in which to display both large and small objects within the room. For those people who love to have their most precious and sentimental possessions around them and always on show, this is the chapter for you – a room scattered with diverse collections of small, eye-catching objects can become a jewel box of visual delights. If your tastes turn to the grander things in life, however, you have not been forgotten – discover how to display large items in a theatrical way and give your room drama. Perhaps surprisingly, simplicity is the key to success with both looks if the finished results are not to grow into the overblown and ridiculous, or degenerate into overheated jumbles of cluttered collections.

showing off | ostentation

In recent years you could be forgiven for feeling that everything in life was weighted towards the understated. Even in the world of fashion, only a few designers put on the gloriously extravagant shows that once captured headlines around the world. A similar trend has taken place in interiors, with many people striving to create environments in which everything blends subtly together. However, if you are one of those people who yearns for an interior with a difference, here are a few tips on how to break through that wall of conformity and make a unique design statement all your own.

There is no doubt that interior design is one of the most efficient mediums for self-expression — our homes are interior, inside, a personal space that we can keep private if we so wish, or into which we can choose to invite others. What you wear, what you say in public and the way you present yourself to the outside world will always be judged by others, but your home can be an interior cocoon where you can exercise any personal foibles and give expression to any individual preoccupations that you desire. So, if you want to be impolitely showy, if you want to make a fuss, the home is the perfect place to do it.

At first thought, creating an ostentatious display might seem an easy thing to do — after all, an ornate candelabrum crowned with flickering flames can grab anyone's attention with ease. However, the point to bear in mind here is that the showpiece of any scheme, while creating a definite impact, should not be so overpowering that it wrests attention completely away from everything else. Instead, you need to achieve a sense of harmony and balance with the rest of the room, so that your dramatic centrepiece becomes a crowning glory rather than a discordant monstrosity.

Another key way of showing off in interiors is to emphasize objects that are normally left understated. The goal is to draw the eye directly and forcefully to what would normally be an insignificant element and, as a result, to delight the eye with both the surprise and the beauty of the display.

MULTIPLE SCULPTURES One bust on a windowsill is, well, one bust on a windowsill. By placing two busts together, however, you can create an emphatic visual statement that draws the eye. Here, an early Victorian doorknocker has been added to the arrangement. Although it is not intellectually related to the classical busts, it is a figurative and highly sculptural element and helps to add weight and therefore a sense of larger scale to the group.

BALANCED CANDLESTICKS Although the two verdigris candlesticks are glorious objects in their own right, they could look stark and lose some of their impact if displayed on their own. An urn has been added to fill the void between them and so create a pleasing U-shaped composition. To give the urn a decorative purpose, it has been filled with lightbulbs to create a pyramid of spheres. The juxtaposition of the bulbs and the candles are a witty but inexpensive way of achieving a richly glamorous effect.

GOLDEN MANTEL
Even such an impressive stone fireplace as this would look lonely if left naked. In order to realize its potential, the mantelshelf has been furnished with ornately framed postcards and a piece of gilded driftwood. The golden theme is picked up in the wallhanging above and the Christmas tree baubles casually laid on the shelf, while the row of tealights echoes the flames of the fire below. The rich, metallic finishes of the various elements turn the fireplace into a dramatic showpiece, but the use of inexpensive items such as postcards and driftwood help to retain a feeling of modernity and spontaneity.

showing off | context

For most of us, the objects with which we decorate our homes are, by and large, of the mundane variety. However beautiful we might think them, unless they are displayed carefully, they can easily blend into the background and go unnoticed. This is particularly true of small objects. The solution to this problem is to draw attention to items by placing them within an eye-catching context. With a little ingenuity, you can create a frame for an object that not only displays it to its best advantage but that also creates a decorating theme to inspire the rest of the room.

SEASIDE SCENE This small but pretty painting has been brought to life by transforming it into a three-dimensional display. The little carved boats look like escapees from the scene behind and make a witty, almost surreal statement that draws the eye to the painting beyond.

CRYSTAL DROPS Drops of crystal can be found at most car boot fairs and junk shops but can be difficult to display effectively. Here, a store-bought wrought-iron chandelier becomes the frame for these tiny objects, which are attached with small lengths of fine wire. The twinkling display looks particularly indulgent and extravagant when placed over a bathtub.

The problem of successfully displaying small or simply less showy objects is one that has occupied interior designers throughout history. Even in the grand homes of the aristocracy, where the objects on display were of great monetary and artistic value, designers were faced with the dilemma of how to draw attention to small and more muted pieces. In fact, it was imperative for designers to find a way of displaying even the smallest of items in a way that reflected their worth and beauty, and hence their owner's prestige and wealth. A mantelshelf weighed down by huge carved bluejohn urns with ormolu mounts might scream for attention, but what about a few worn-stone archaeological fragments? An enormous and priceless old master painting hung on a wall opposite a doorway might draw the eye across the expanse of a huge hall, but how could an exquisite but tiny Renaissance cameo capture attention?

Today, the objects with which we embellish our homes are rarely worth a great deal in economic terms but they can be of immense sentimental value – a small painting bought during a honeymoon, for example, can retain its charm and evoke wonderful memories in years to come if displayed with care. It is well worth looking through some illustrated books or magazines of historic houses and palaces for ideas, or visiting them if possible – you may sigh with envy but you will also find a thousand and one display solutions that are still relevant today. It all boils down to having a keen eye for composition and investing a degree of trial and error into finding the best way to show less prestigious items off to their best advantage.

style lab | mirrors

Space and cost constraints often mean that modern interiors are composed of small rooms, frequently with very little natural light. One solution to this problem is to use large mirrors to reflect and magnify the light and to increase the feeling of space. In addition, using elements that are deliberately too big for a room can help to make a grand statement.

INCREASING DEPTH The sloping ceilings of this attic room are naturally restrictive, so a large mirror propped in a corner confuses the eye into believing that there is another room beyond.

INCREASING HEIGHT The obvious, traditional place for a large mirror is above a fireplace. This extends the space upwards and makes low ceilings feel lofty. To modernize this traditional display, nothing has been placed around the mirror in order to achieve a simple, uncluttered look.

MAXIMIZING COLOUR For this modern apartment, with its exciting architectural detailing and contemporary colour palette, a large mirror propped against one wall reflects a variety of elements in a range of different colours. This enlivens the small space by appearing to increase the spread of colour, and once again confuses the eye into believing that the space is larger than it really is.

MAXIMIZING DAYLIGHT A mirror is the perfect way to maximize the amount of light in a room. It is particularly useful in an urban apartment, which generally receives light reflected from other buildings. A mirror placed near a window maximizes the small amount of daylight that can find a doglegged course between the houses opposite and into the room.

Very often the objects with which we furnish our homes are too large for the context in which we place them. This may be due to having inherited an unsuitably sized item, having to make do with gifts from friends and relatives when first setting up home, or simply having a faulty memory of the space available when purchasing something new. Whatever the cause, however, there are plenty of solutions.

STANDARD LAMP
This is a nicely carved, mid-20th-century oak standard lamp with a cunningly integrated tray table. Originally it would have been topped with an enormous and ornate drum shade, probably peppered with violently coloured flowers. Here, a simple cream shade with a slight camber readjusts the proportions to ensure that the lamp does not dominate the space under a very low ceiling.

Our great grandparents would probably be shocked at the smallness of the spaces we inhabit compared with their own. Even the more modestly sized family houses that were built at the end of the 19th century are now routinely downsized and converted into a series of tiny apartments. However, although the spaces in which we live are much reduced, many of us still have a generous taste in furniture and, of course, some items just cannot be greatly decreased in size if they are to remain functional.

Old furniture is a particular problem since it was designed to harmonize with high ceilings and broad planes of wall. Provided something fits through the door, all too often we are satisfied. However, care must be taken if large objects are not to dominate a scheme and make everything else in the room appear ridiculously small. Once again, it is context that can help, and any trick that can be used to soften the blow or blur the edges is fair game.

SIDEBOARD Although extremely useful, if left unchecked this sideboard could steal the show, so the proportions have been readjusted by placing a tall chair on either side. The height of the chairs has been stretched by painting motifs on the wall above them in the same pale green colour. These look almost like crests for the chairs, which make the chairs appear taller and the sideboard shorter.

Picture frames are designed to emphasize pictures. They act as a border to separate the picture from the wall and to draw the eye into the intricacies of the painted, printed or drawn surface. The same principle can be applied to the architecture of the room itself.

Before the modernists prescribed that doors should be mere openings in a wall and that windows should be brutally cut apertures designed solely to let in the light, the architectural openings in a room were emphasized by heavily moulded architraves. Architraves also served the practical purpose of protecting brittle plaster from knocks and scrapes. Other features of interior architecture such as fireplaces would receive a design treatment different from the rest of the room in order to draw the eye towards them and create a more emphatic design statement.

Rooms that have undersized or oversized architectural elements can be rebalanced using a series of easy solutions that either shrink the overscaled or increase the underscaled. The key is to judge the proportions of the room objectively. People so often believe, erroneously, that architectural elements such as skirtings or dado rails should always be of a particular height. New dado rails are generally fitted at around 1 metre (3 feet) above the floor, which can be far too high for a modern room with a low ceiling. The height of the dado should in fact be one third of whatever the height of the room is, and the height of the skirting should be approximately one quarter of the space below the dado. This will create a harmonious series of classical proportions.

FIREPLACE SURROUND This fireplace was far too small for the living room in which it is situated, so a large pale-coloured border has been painted around it to increase the visual weight of the undersized surround.

WINDOWFRAME This window is wide but not very high. Hanging blinds from the top of the frame would make the window appear even shorter, so simple canvas dummy blinds (fixed permanently in this position rather than intended for use) have been hung directly beneath the ceiling in order to increase the height of the window and make the proportion of glass to wall more harmonious.

MINIMAL WINDOW BAY The original architecture of this bow-ended drawing room is undeniably stunning. In its heyday, the space would have been a riot of richly coloured and heavily draped damask fabrics. Today's occupants have used the bare minimum of furniture arranged in a rigid symmetry to bring the room alive while allowing the natural beauty of the architecture to remain the undisputed feature of the room. Gold- and bronze-coloured paints were rubbed over the surface of the ornate ceiling cornice to create an instantly eye-catching architectural frame.

architectural frames | embellishing

Late 1960s and early 1970s interior designers hit upon the idea of creating a 'feature' wall. They felt that using dense pattern or rich colour throughout a scheme would be excessive and so restricted themselves to embellishing just a single important, or feature, wall. The same idea can still be used successfully today.

Although the original purveyors of the feature wall idea used it *ad nauseam*, it is basically a good design principle that can be resurrected in the modern interior to emphasize a specific plane within the room. You do, however, have to be careful about the type of contrasts you create between the feature wall and the remaining surfaces. Those of us who grew up during the feature wall's heyday can all remember instances where the idea went dramatically wrong — nightmare visions of five different wallpapers all used in the same room (and all scarily unrelated to each other).

Rooms today are generally on the small side and without any interesting architectural features, so restricting areas of richness to a chimney breast, for example, is a good way to make the space seem bigger. Walls painted or papered with a flat, neutral treatment will appear to recede, while heavy colours or weighty patterns will seem to force their way forwards. A room that is completely neutral can be a visual nonentity; a room that is full of ornamentation can become a staccato box. Ideally, play one look off against the other. In this way, a patterned chimney breast will visually come towards you while the neutral walls around it will move farther away; the two together emphasize this effect to make the room seem bigger.

COLOUR BLOCKS Orderly but random geometric shapes in closely related, muted colours create soft and understated interest either side of a chimney breast. The effect was achieved using small tester pots of paint, a spirit level and masking tape.

STRIPES AND BLOCKS The bold, vertical colours on the chimney breast, painted in a random series of stripes, make the ceiling feel higher, while the horizontal bands in the rest of the room push the corners away and make the width of the space appear broader and lower.

small collections | attracting attention

The eye is often drawn to tiny objects that twinkle and sparkle, or that simply have a wealth of intricate detail for the eye to explore and delight in. If seen individually, there is hardly anything to appreciate but, when arranged in a group, the objects meld together to make a cohesive whole.

In a way the most effective thing you could do to show off a group of small objects is display them behind a giant magnifying lens. For the average interior, however, this is probably a little over the top – most people want their homes to look inviting, not like a private museum – but the basic principle can be adapted quite easily to create a stylish, contemporary look. For example, small waterproof items such as beads, buttons, pebbles or seashells could be placed inside a glass vase filled with water, which will act like a magnifying glass.

A more practical way to display a group of small objects is to place them in an appropriate context that will help draw the eye towards the tiny focal points – small shells in an expanse of sand, for example. You can also create a structural frame for the collection that will focus attention on the objects within. The frame and the collection do not have to be related; in fact, the more unusual the relationship between the two, the more successful the design statement will often be. Another option is to use small collections as decorative elements with which to embellish an entirely unrelated object, so that both items are displayed to best effect.

CUTLERY TRAY FRAME Little handblown glass animals disporting themselves in a variety of witty tableaux are fragile and insubstantial visually. Both of these display constraints have been answered by arranging them in an upended cutlery tray that acts as an unusual but effective frame.

DOLL'S HOUSE FURNITURE Beautifully detailed miniature furniture can be wasted if hidden inside a doll's house. Here, it has been arranged in the open, inside the indented block of a bookshelf, which provides the perfect frame. To increase visibility so that the details of the collection can be fully appreciated, the display has been staggered by placing some of the items on top of blocks of acrylic at different heights.

PYRAMID OF DOLLS When a collection is of a uniform height, it is a good idea to break the outline and create a pyramid composition. These porcelain doll's bodies – all whimsical prettiness – are ideally suited to the plinths on which they stand, which are in fact wedding-cake tier supports.

DISH OF MARBLES Simple solutions should never be overlooked. A large white meat dish on a tabletop makes a neutral backdrop for a collection of old and new marbles. The exotic colours and minute bubbles in the cast glass of the marbles create dramatic reflections, coloured shadows and flickering, bouncing highlights on the plate.

BUTTON LAMPSHADE A collection of pretty buttons might seem almost impossible to display but here they have been glued onto a lampshade in a random, all-over pattern. Buttons made of horn, mother-of-pearl or Bakelite are translucent enough to allow light to pass through them.

SHELLS IN SAND These tiny shells were collected from rock pools during a seaside holiday. However, pretty though they may be, they would go unnoticed if simply placed on a shelf. Instead, they have been inserted into a complementary setting of sand to produce a miniature Japanese-style display. A chopstick was used to create waves in the sand to enhance the seaside context; the curls of the wooden sticks rising behind the plate reflect this undulating rhythm.

photographs | framing

It always seems such a shame to consign photographs to albums when they can bring joy into the home if incorporated into our living spaces. Whether they are placed unobtrusively around the room so that you catch glimpses of them now and again as you move about, or whether they are situated directly within the line of concentrated vision when sitting or eating, photographs can help stamp your personality onto your home as well as enhance an interior scheme with the aesthetic value of the images themselves.

The easiest way to display photographs is to place them in a suitable frame that can be hung on a wall or stood on a surface. There are no hard and fast rules about what type of frame will work best, so you need to take care when choosing. Some photographs will look wonderful surrounded by ornate silver, while others look best displayed in a plain, contemporary box frame; similarly, some photographs will be enhanced by a neutral-coloured frame but others will only burst into life when surrounded by vibrant colour. It is a case of trial and error, depending on the type of photograph you want to display, the interior scheme of the room where the picture is to be placed and the overall effect that you are aiming to create.

If you want to display a collection of photographs, frames can be an expensive option. In addition, a wall of framed photographs can make the individual pictures blend into one another and reduce the impact of each of the images. Instead, you can integrate groups of photographs into an interior scheme by using them to embellish items of furniture such as a screen, table or lampshade.

SCREEN Display screens are now widely available and are ideal for showing off photographs. For added impact, the photographs in this screen were photocopied and taped into position without a backboard. Photocopies are fairly translucent and, if placed in front of a window, as here, light can pass through them to illuminate the images.

GLASS-TOPPED TABLE This is a very simple sideways solution to displaying photographs. Except for its orientation, a glass-topped table functions in exactly the same way as a photograph frame but has the additional benefit of providing a useful surface on which to display other items.

LAMPSHADE Photocopies of photographs have been pasted onto this lampshade using dilute PVA adhesive. The adhesive dries to a hard finish when pasted over both the back and front of the copy and increases the translucency of the images.

style lab | postcards

Postcards are an economical way of bringing your favourite art into your home. Although postcards are by their nature on the small side, they can be displayed in a variety of ways to create artpieces with impact. Their small format need not be an impediment to their design potential – never forget that 'downscale' postcards can easily be turned into 'upscale' colour photocopies.

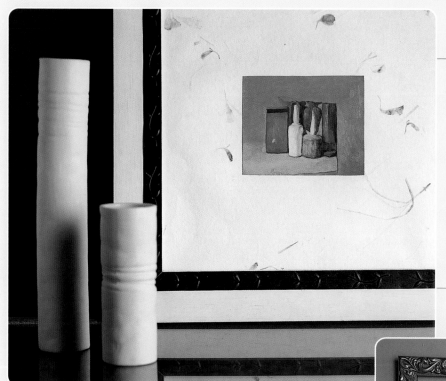

SMALL IMAGE, LARGE FRAME
Framing a small image inside a large mount is a popular decorative device. The acres of plain mount make the small postcard seem more valuable. You could use a series of similar pictures framed in this way to fill a blank wall, creating a sophisticated design scheme that relies on the repeated rhythm of the pictures within the frames for its impact.

MULTIPLE IMAGES Here, several postcards have been stuck directly onto the wall, leaving plenty of the wall paint to frame the images. The old gilt frame creates an ornate border around the collection. The joy of sticking the postcards directly onto the wall using removable adhesive is that they can easily be changed if they fall out of favour, or if you wish to create a different mood in a room for a particular occasion.

THREE-DIMENSIONAL DISPLAY

Enlarging a postcard image is easy to do using a photocopier. This enlarged still life painting has been stuck to the back of a box frame. The full display potential of the frame has been explored by placing a small antique bottle within it, creating a real-life foreground to the painted still life behind.

HOUSE OF CARDS

Postcards can, believe it or not, achieve a sculptural presence if you have steady enough hands to build a house of cards. This is a lovely way of combining several different images and can be made to last by sticking the edges of the cards in place using a hot glue gun. A house of cards makes a striking centrepiece for a table or a vertical feature on a mantelshelf or windowsill. Collections of smaller objects such as pebbles, marbles or buttons can find an aesthetic home on the postcard edifice.

china | grouping by pattern

Many people derive a great deal of pleasure from collecting china. We are instinctively driven to assemble 'sets' of things and, with the popularity of searching for treasures at car boot sales and antiques markets, having a goal or quest increases the fun of the chase. It is, however, very much up to you to define what composes a set. Is it elements from the same dinner service or are you flexible enough to opt simply for colour or pattern themes? Certainly, you will find it easier to create a successful display the more adaptable you are.

Go into any traditional country house hotel and you will more than likely find an interior scheme bursting with pattern upon pattern upon pattern. You will encounter a vista of floral curtains contorted through a series of tiebacks and pelmets, hanging against papered walls with a different pattern above and below the dado, leading down to a carpet spinning with a thousand vines, upon which stands a draped table supporting a pyramid of patterned china. The result is utterly overwhelming. However, if you remove, simplify, edit and paint everything except the china an ivory colour, you will have a pretty interior scheme where the pattern of the china reigns supreme.

A grouping of china need not share a common date or origin provided the patterns rhyme among themselves. You do not have to restrict yourself to exactly the same pattern, either. In fact, not doing so will provide an enhanced palette of forms with which to create exciting compositions full of dramatic changes in scale and exhilaratingly broken outlines. It also means that old and new can be combined to make a more individual statement about your own design personality. What goes well together is not an exact science but similar colours and shades as well as related motifs are good starting points. After that, an afternoon of relaxed trial and error will always unearth a successful solution.

BLUE AND WHITE CHINA Blue and white is a classic china combination. These eclectic mixes of old and new china are brought together by a shared colour scheme and traditional decorative theme.

VICTORIAN FLORAL CHINA The delicate prettiness of the floral pattern and the sprinkling of gilt highlights unite this collection of china objects. The fact that they do not match exactly makes a charming and informal statement that underplays the grand origins of the pieces. The patterned cushion provides an informal backdrop to the display.

CHRYSANTHEMUM WARE Although not a set, the pair of vases on the left and the rose bowl on the right were both decorated using the same technique, so although the rose bowl is much older and of finer quality, it sits well with the vases. Dried roses in the bowl and fresh roses in the vases link the pieces further.

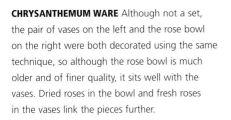

This chapter is all about dealing with the clutter of everyday family life. A well-designed home should not be a showpiece, with an intimidating succession of perfect interiors that require constant maintenance. There has to be room for fun, for enjoyment for the whole family, no matter how untidy they may be. As many of us know from first-hand experience, 'practicality', 'pets', 'children' and 'partners' can have a seemingly God-given ability to rain on our aesthetic parade. Left to our own devices, of course, everything in the home would be gorgeously arranged, terrifyingly tidy and every object would have its own special beauty – or that's the theory most of us delude ourselves with, anyway. Even if living on your own, however, you are bound to possess a range of

generation | game

less-than-lovely but essential items that have to be accommodated. When you have a family, of course, those items are multiplied and the space in which to deal with them reduced. So what solutions are there? Well, you really have only two choices. You can either give up the ghost and abandon all style for the sake of family harmony, or take the bull by the horns and absorb everybody's detritus with some cunning tricks and grown-up solutions. If you choose the former option, fine; but why settle for a clutter-filled home when you could so easily disguise that clutter and sometimes even turn it into an attractive display in its own right? Basically, there is no reason why you cannot have your design cake and eat it, provided you adopt a certain degree of aesthetic lateral thinking.

stylish barbies | childish clutter

Children these days seem to have an eye for design – perhaps they always had. Certainly, most teenagers have very strong opinions about how they want their bedrooms to be decorated. Tidiness, however, never seems to be one of a child's requirements. With just a handful of toys, even the best-behaved children can create a tidal wave of clutter that can swamp a nicely arranged interior.

Of course, if you are one of those semi-fictional characters who has enough space for a separate children's playroom, childish clutter can be consigned to that area. Back in the real world, however, most of us have to accommodate children and their attendant wake of broken toys into our already painfully contracted living spaces and, as a result, an unending war develops. Obviously, as adults, we are bigger and brainier, so we should be able to win the war – even if we do lose the occasional battle.

One of the best weapons in our armoury against childish clutter is storage. Storage space in a cupboard, chest or other container is the most obvious solution. It is important that this space is easy to access so that toys can simply be thrown in and out as and when they are needed. For those items that seem to be in constant use, perhaps the best thing to do is to brush them into a corner of the room at the end of the day and place a screen in front.

Design-clever parents can involve the children in the origination of these storage solutions so that they instantly feel part of the 'putting away' protocol that heralds bedtime. Children are funny creatures – ask them to clear away their belongings and a tantrum could ensue, but fool them into believing that tidying up is the final act of their game and they will be sweetness itself. Similarly, if they themselves have been responsible for the embellishment of a screen or toy chest, they could be more likely to use it.

SHOEBOXES

Shoeboxes are ideal night-time resting places for toys after the children have gone to bed. They are fairly tough and resilient, and can be decorated in a variety of ways: covered with sticky-back plastic in a design of your choice (left); decoupaged with photocopied images (above); or covered with wallpaper and varnished with acrylic (above left).

SCREEN Whoever said there was anything wrong with a bit of sweeping under the carpet? The simplest and easiest antidote to childish clutter is simply to screen off the evidence. You could even buy your child a mini-broom so that they can join in the game. There are many different screens available to buy but they are actually very easy to make. The requisite hinges and sheets of timber are readily available from DIY stores, and your child can then decorate this blank canvas however they wish (under your aesthetic supervision, of course).

If you have children, you need to be resolutely practical about the situation. Instead of trying to hide all of the childish clutter, why not absorb some it and turn it into a display? A shelf of higgledy-piggledy plastic dolls will never delight the eye but facing them all in the same direction, adjusting their dresses to preserve their modesty and flattening their hair to add a touch of style is often enough to work aesthetic wonders.

ARTWORK DISPLAY

A neat, flexible solution to displaying children's artwork is to make a special display board. Here, a piece of MDF was cut to size and covered with an offcut of the wallpaper used in the rest of the room. A sheet of Perspex was then cut to the same size and drilled so that it could be fixed to the wooden backboard using chrome-capped screws. Artworks can then be posted between the Perspex and wood. If maximum density is reached and the Perspex completely saturated by hand prints and potato cuts, simply loosen the screws, remove the existing paintings and insert new ones. Generally speaking, for the price of a sheet of Perspex (minimal), a piece of MDF (negligible) and a handful of screws (almost insignificant), you can create a large, impressive modern frame.

Bravely facing the realities of the situation is a great step forward — as far as children's toys go, that reality is often brightly coloured and made exclusively of plastic. Children seem incapable of even considering gorgeously hand-carved wooden toys in lieu of the latest 'as seen on TV' instrument of playtime torture. That, however, should not stop you from buying that delicious naive sheep on wheels for yourself — and, if that one gorgeous object happens to find itself poking out of the top of the open toy box rather than a one-armed 'Action Boy' or 'Baby Blue Deirdre' with singed hair, then you can instantly chalk up a partial victory. The children are still there, the evidence still abounds, but your eye is drawn to something that gives you pleasure rather than a shudder of mass-produced revulsion. The key to success, therefore, is compromise.

In order to turn your children's toys or other collections of objects into displays, you need to find some kind of context or frame in which to place them that is sympathetic with the main decoration of the room. Apart from toys, of course, children love to produce their own artworks. These come in a variety of sizes, shapes, colours and, it has to be said, qualities. Pinboards get tatty very quickly and the heavy poster paint used for most children's paintings means that the pictures soon curl like autumn leaves, so it is often best to frame the artworks — but again, you need to do this in a way that is sympathetic with the rest of the room.

NATURE TABLE This printer's tray was covered with cut-to-size Perspex and placed on top of an old drawer unit to become a repository for a childish collection of precious objects. From organizing pebbles to plastic figurines, the child will begin to see the attraction of order from chaos. If you cannot find a printer's tray, antique or modern cutlery trays can be called on as a substitute.

out of harm's reach | crockery and china

Delicate, easily broken objects are forever a beautiful liability. Many people feel that having children and lovely china in the same room is a recipe for disaster and, as a result, anything remotely breakable, no matter how well loved, gets tucked away in a box at the back of a cupboard until the children have grown. However, with a little care and forethought, it is perfectly possible to display delicate objects in the same room as children without spending half your life snatching china tureens from impending toddler doom.

By far the most obvious solution to the problem is to place breakable items of crockery high out of reach. This is an area in which previous generations of designers and architects excelled. Just a century or two ago, architects often built specific places for china display within a room; for example, recessed cupboards on either side of a fireplace and deep mantelshelves. The Victorians, who loved to show off as many objects as possible, often built deep shelves above the picture rail, which they quickly filled with a clutter of china. The outer edge of the shelf often had a shallow groove so that plates could be stood vertically, hence the term 'plate shelf'. These were popular right into the 1940s, when a romanticized, 'cottagey' look reached its zenith of popularity. The Georgians loved big collections of china divided into compositional groups – a pair of tall vases, two round pots, candlesticks and perhaps a planter. These are sometimes called 'garnitures' and comprised matching sets. Formal arrangements were often displayed on mantelshelves, while deep cornices above doorframes were a popular site for garnitures. Mingling dinner china, vases or figurines with books in a bookcase has an eclectic appeal that still holds true today.

CHINA SHELF Bookshelves need not be solely for books. This fitted bookcase separates a kitchen from a dining room and, as such, is an ideal place for storing the dinner service. A variety of white china objects placed in front of the plates create compositional uprights in front of the repetitive rhythm of the round plates. Junk shop china, as here, rarely comes in pairs, but it is still possible to create a symmetrical arrangement with them; the non-symmetry of the objects has the added benefit of keeping the display subtly informal.

SHAKER PEG RAIL The universal popularity of Shaker style has revived the fortunes of the peg rail. Practically speaking, in china storage terms, the peg rail is normally only one step up from that 1970s horror, the mug tree. Here, however, difficult-to-display china pieces such as a tureen have been hung from the rail with sash cord in a manner inspired by 17th-century Spanish still lifes.

You either love ornaments or hate them. Those who hate them believe that little pieces of pretty but ultimately useless china damn an interior to perpetual frumpiness; others would find a home without ornaments unwelcoming, unfinished and without aesthetic appeal. Where children are concerned, the ornament issue is only problematic because it is not easy to find a suitable perch for a porcelain figurine that is out of harm's reach while still retaining its visual impact.

Most people's rooms are flat-faced boxes, with the only architectural relief in this cuboid space provided by a chimney breast or bay window. Our natural instinct is to furnish our flat walls with flat objects such as mirrors or framed pictures. The daring might flirt with an additional half dimension and suspend the odd plate, but we largely forget about the decorative potential of three-dimensional objects displayed on wall-hung plinths.

Bracket shelves designed to take a single object are an efficient and practical solution to raising a breakable heirloom or junk shop indulgence above the range of clumsy toddler fingers. On an aesthetic level, they cast shadows across a flat wall surface that can create an additional dimension of interest.

Traditional decorating derived from Georgian principles relies on pyramids of wall-hung objects that might start with a pair of framed prints, rise into a heavy, round, framed mirror and reach an apex in a vase with a curvy outline displayed on a bracket shelf. If the principle is simplified, the shapes tailored and the objects chosen with a contemporary eye, a modern effect can also be achieved.

CONTEMPORARY BOX SHELF Pictures in frames or framed mirrors are obvious ways of bringing walls to life, but three-dimensional objects on small shelves answer two problems: obviously, a china vase on a shelf is out of harm's reach, but it can also provide a sculptural focus that breaks up a flat wall. On the page opposite, an interestingly shaped opaque green glass vase has been placed on a contemporary box shelf (opposite, below). The shelf itself is made from pieces of MDF screwed together and fixed to the wall with a mirror plate, then painted in the same colour as the wall. Be careful when using such shelves: heavy objects are not advisable for this kind of delicate arrangement. Despite its contemporary feel, the same shelf is just as effective for displaying more classical objects, such as an early Victorian urn (opposite, above).

ORNATE GILDED SHELF In the picture above, a fret-cut MDF bracket from a DIY store was sprayed gold and a delicate semicircular MDF shelf screwed onto the top. The effect is romantic, almost fairytale-like, and is perfectly complemented by the sweet cherub vase bought cheaply in a junk shop.

style lab | family photographs

Displaying your relatives in ornate silver on the glossy black lid of a piano is a tried and trusted cliché. However, if you don't happen to have a piano or the budget for silver but you do have some nice family photographs, there are alternatives.

ORNATE FRAME This old photograph of a relative has been treated like fine art and placed in an ornate gilt frame. To soften the look and subvert any pomposity, the picture is stood simply on a shelf next to a vase containing a hedgerow flower.

WIRE AND PEGS The delicate sepia of the original photograph has been reproduced in these photocopies, which have been attached to tensioned wire with silver pegs in an ultra contemporary space. The juxtaposition of the old and the modern draws the attention and produces an interesting and successful display.

SIMPLE FRAME Here, a simple frame without a mount has been used; the photograph was stuck directly onto the wall using removable adhesive. The delicate buff colour of the old picture's edge is incorporated into the scheme to act as an inner frame that echoes the light colour of the wooden frame. The overall effect is like that of a modern box frame, which gives a subtle contemporary twist to an old image.

POP ART In this instance, the photograph has been photocopied onto sheets of acetate (most good photocopy shops now offer this service) and the backs roughly coloured with bright acrylic paints to create a homemade pop art-inspired extravaganza.

coats, bags & shoes | inspired storage

Why is it that coat cupboards just never seem to be big enough to accommodate everyone's outer garments and footwear? To solve the problem of the overflow, or in the absence of a hall cupboard altogether, finding a suitable way of storing these items in the hallway is a necessity but, since they will more than likely have to remain on view, a deliberate effort will be required to maintain order.

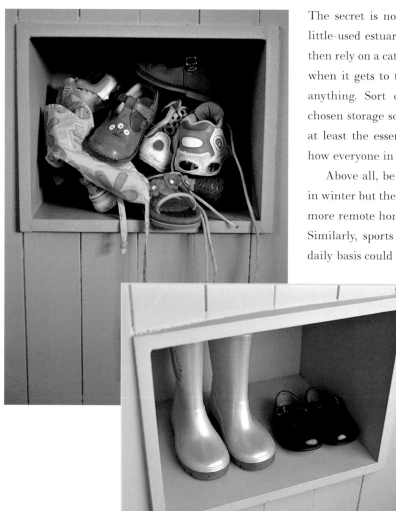

The secret is not to let the area silt up like a little-used estuary over a period of months and then rely on a cataclysmic frenzy of organization when it gets to the stage that nobody can find anything. Sort out your solution, design the chosen storage so that there is enough space for at least the essentials and keep a daily eye on how everyone in the family uses the space.

Above all, be ruthless. Boots may be needed in winter but they could easily be found another, more remote home during the summer months. Similarly, sports shoes that are not used on a daily basis could just as easily live in the bottom of the wardrobe in the bedroom. Since children's feet grow so rapidly, pass on anything outgrown as soon as you can rather than allow cast-off footwear to take up precious hallway space.

Remember, too, that there can be a simple beauty even in everyday objects providing they are deliberately arranged. The Shakers were cunning in their quest for simplicity and Shaker peg rails are perfect for hanging outdoor wear. Rather than having a mish-mash of things hanging from the rail, however, why not put trainers, mittens, scarves, dog leads and so on into pretty drawstring bags (which are very easy to make) so that the coat rack is reclaimed as a decorative item rather than being reduced to a purely utilitarian one.

CUBBYHOLE SHOEBOX This indented cubbyhole in a hallway (opposite) was a good place to store shoes but obviously began to lose its way when the family started throwing all their footwear inside with no thought for order. A ruthless edit and the effect is transformed.

COAT HOOKS Coat hooks with different personalities take everyone back to primary school and give each individual their own designated hanging space as well as the responsibility for keeping it tidy. For the obsessives among us, the obvious next step would be the addition of nameplates.

generation | game

WARDROBE ART If you are really proud of an outfit and wake up in the morning longing to put on a particular item of clothing, it seems a shame to keep it out of sight behind the wardrobe door. Interior designers have long realized the decorative potential of garments in a room scheme – the glossy magazines are more than likely to have at least one project every month that has a kimono or ethnic head-dress used successfully as part of an interior decoration. Shoes and handbags, so often objects of real desire, lend themselves particularly well to becoming interior ornaments thanks to their sculptural shapes and decorative details.

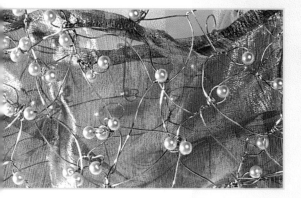

COLOUR THEMES AND TEXTURES

So often when a space has just been decorated, the finished effect can feel flat and uninspiring because it has little detail – few elements on which the eye can pleasurably rest. Shopping your way out of an aesthetic crisis is one solution but another, simpler approach is to look around and see whether you own anything suitable. Raiding the wardrobe or chest of drawers can prove hugely fruitful, particularly since our taste in clothes will often blend well with our taste in interiors. Look for elements that will harmonize with the colours of the scheme while adding much-needed texture.

Now that the immediate family members have been dealt with, it's time to sort out the extended family: those furry-faced friends that delight our days with unquestioning loyalty but clutter our kitchens with paraphernalia. Most pets need their own bed, but these tend to be fairly mundane and often downright unattractive. However, a judicious makeover can transform even the dullest of doggy dens, though you must take care not to use any products that may be dangerous to the animal.

When pet beds are made of gorgeously crafted willow they are a delight to behold, but seasoned dog owners know all too well that the pet in question is more likely to misconstrue such a bed as a cunningly convenient tooth-sharpening implement rather than a place to sleep. That is why most of us choose resilient plastic pet beds that can be hosed out after unfortunate accidents and will survive an enthusiastic chew largely unharmed. Plastic beds, however, are usually ugly. So, too, are most rabbit hutches and rodent cages, but there are things you can do to remedy the situation.

Before embarking on a makeover of your pet's living quarters, you must make sure that the design and products you intend to use will not be harmful to the animal. Check all paint labels carefully and, if you have any doubts, speak to an advisor at your local pet store. Generally, it is safe to transform plastic beds with enamel or car paints (provided they are not lead-based). If you cannot find a safe paint, you could line the bed with an attractive blanket or rug that will detract from the plastic beneath. The seasoned timber of rabbit hutches can be transformed with exterior paints, wood dyes or stains (restrict your design efforts to the outside of the hutch).

Another consideration to take into account when designing the living space of your pet is how to accommodate the various other items that come as part of the package, such as leads, chew toys and so on. The best answer is to create some easily accessible but attractive storage that can be displayed alongside more aesthetic objects – not necessarily pet-related – to create a harmonious whole.

PAISLEY DOG BED Either this pet has delusions of grandeur or it's the campest poodle in the park. Enamel spray paint has been used to transform this ordinary pet bed into the doggy version of a chaise longue, while the aesthetic *coup de grace* – gold paisley – comes courtesy of a figured stamp and gold enamel paint.

RABBIT HUTCH Pretty pastel checks in hardwearing exterior paints have transformed the outside of this rabbit hutch. The decoration of the hutch is relatively superficial but, if you think your pet deserves something more extravagant, then let your imagination run riot – why not add a few turrets using exterior-grade plywood?

PET CLUTTER

Keeping everything close to where it is needed – by your pet's bed – is an obvious practical decision. Here, lidded baskets have been used to hold doggy necessities such as leads and biscuits. The basket of hyacinth bulbs lends a decorative edge.

As children we could always count on certain reactions from our parents. Without fail, their faces would adopt a gloomy downward thrust when presented with our excitement at having brought home from a fair a goldfish in a plastic bag filled with water. Why? Gloom at the impending doom of the new fish's expected early demise and gloom at having to find a suitable home for it in the meantime.

Fish in tanks were the ultimate exoticism in the 1960s and 1970s. James Bond's foe Doctor No, with his magnifying aquaria and vividly coloured subaquatic friends, launched a thousand room features of a similar nature. Keeping tropical fish is a high-maintenance, high-expenditure hobby, but the simple little everyday goldfish in its bowl is a different matter altogether.

It is worth stressing here that the welfare of the fishy inhabitants of those bowls is the most important consideration. A quick chat with a fish expert at your local pet store or a flick through a fish-keeping guide is a good way of allaying any anxieties you may have regarding the required living conditions. Once you have done that, you can then immerse yourself in devising different ways to make a fish in a tank look ravishing on your mantelshelf.

Finding a glass container with an unusual shape immediately makes a bold style statement – there are plenty of attractive vases available that are large enough to accommodate a single goldfish. Then comes the question of furnishing your fish's home. If a goldfish can be happy in a bowl with some gravel and a plastic mermaid,

FASHIONABLE FISH

Fish need somewhere to hide, so why not go for something unusual such as a bright teacup and saucer (near right)? As long as the object is not going to dissolve in water, it will be safe. If you like the idea of a fishbowl but you don't have – or want to look after – a real fish, there are plenty of floating fake ones that can be suspended in the tank of your choice (far right).

surely it would achieve aesthetic heights of delight to find itself in a stylish glass vase furnished with a more unusual but infinitely more decorative collection of objects? These must, of course, be safe but that does not mean they have to be plastic effigies of a sunken pirate ship.

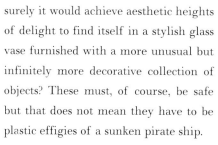

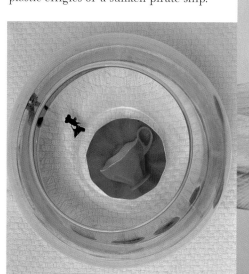

NATURAL FISHBOWL
If your tastes run to a more naturally furnished fishbowl arrangement rather than the more brightly coloured variety, clean garden or seaside pebbles or shells will always look good with a goldfish swimming above. If you need to aerate the tank, anchor the appropriate plants to the pebbles or use them to hide the necessary equipment to keep your fish breathing happily in its watery abode.

technology | blending

Let's face it: on returning home after a hard day at work, all that most of us want to do is settle down in a comfy chair and enjoy a pleasant but undemanding evening watching television. Equipment such as TVs, CD players and computers are now seen as essential items and, since we use them so much, they are generally placed prominently within the room. A great deal of care must be taken, therefore, if they are not to become a technological eyesore in an otherwise desirable interior.

Technology is one of the realities of modern life. Another reality is that the aesthetic design of most items of technology leaves much to be desired. Our commitment to and reliance on technology is peculiar to our age, and many people find it difficult to integrate it successfully into a design scheme. We have no historical aesthetic precedents to follow since the items of technology on which we rely for entertainment have a design tradition that stretches back only a couple of generations. This, of course, is completely at odds with the rest of our homes, since most of us possess a variety of items whose designs originate from past centuries – the items themselves may be brand new but the designs on which they are based are not. You need to be prepared to put a few hours of creative thought into resolving the problem in order to achieve a successful aesthetic compromise.

There are two avenues to explore. You could go for the simplistic look – hide the TV, cloak the CD player and store the computer in a cupboard. Most furniture stores stock a variety of cabinets into which a TV or other piece of technological equipment can be hidden. The alternative is to look closely at the electronic object in question, assess its form, colour and finish, then place it in a complementary context with the right styling so that it will blend into the room. This does not mean that you have to transform the rest of the room into a chrome and black leather palace in order to match the item of technology. Instead, you could concentrate on the squareness of the television, for example, and create a setting that has a similar formality and symmetry into which the TV will comfortably fit.

COMPUTER CUPBOARD If you are having cupboards fitted, why not explore the possibility of integrating technology within? This way, you can have the flexibility of bringing the equipment into the room only when needed. Here, a computer in a cupboard is mounted on a pull-out shelf on drawer runners so that it can be slid out when required.

CD PLAYER Good design has to marry aesthetics with logistics. Here, the ideal place for a CD player from the practical point of view – on a table behind the sofa – has been turned to design advantage. The player itself is placed centrally and framed with neatly stacked CDs on either side, which create a horizontal visual link with the paired table lamps. Changing CDs can then be comfortably achieved from a reclining position without compromising the sophisticated atmosphere of the scheme.

Until the second half of the 20th century, the heart of any living room was the warmth and light of the fire. These days, however, it is the television that the family gathers around in the evenings. The square black box that dominates the family home may be a fact of modern life but it need not be a design embarrassment. If handled like any other piece of furniture, there is no reason why your television should not enhance the room.

TRADITIONAL SETTING This television has been placed on a secondhand Lloyd Loom chest that has been re-covered in black silk. Two mahogany urns on pedestals either side of the arrangement instantly create a symmetrical Georgian feel that tricks the eye into reading the television set as a black box rather than a modern piece of technology.

SURREAL FRAME This might look a bit surreal but, in a funny sort of way, it is a very honest piece of display. The television is now the main focus of most living rooms and, by framing it in this way, it becomes an interesting design feature as well as an object of focus.

MODERN SCREEN Folding screens do not have to be solid in design. Here, contemporary fret-cut wood has been hinged to create a screen that takes the eye away from the television but without shrinking the room by entirely blocking the space.

ANTIQUE SCREEN For inflexible technophobes who really cannot bear having the 21st century in their living rooms, the television needs to be disguised. Hiding it in a television cabinet can cause difficulties, particularly in small rooms, since this large piece of furniture needs to be set at an angle in the room and can overpower everything else. A simpler solution is to invest in an old firescreen that can be moved around to suit.

sports | paraphernalia

Most families possess a range of sports items: balls of various kinds, racquets, golf clubs and so on. Unless you have unlimited cupboard space, this paraphernalia has to be accommodated in the interior scheme in some way, especially if it is in regular use. Unfortunately, although modern sports equipment is a vast improvement on its forebears in terms of function, this is not the case in the realm of aesthetic appeal.

As with the clutter of children's toys, so with sports equipment: it needs to be absorbed into the design scheme of the room. Again, the first rule is to keep it tidy. Coming up fast on the inside track is the need to distract the eye. Modern golf clubs never seem to have the same mellow splendour as those used by our grandparents, so it is necessary to incorporate them into a display that removes the emphasis from any offending elements. The same can also be said of tennis racquets. These days sporty things seem to look just a little bit too, well, sporty — all go-faster stripes and sweat-resistant grips. Basically, it is all a bit too professional to sit easily within the home.

If your life just cannot continue without a collection of golf clubs by the front door, then rely on a little visual sleight of hand to get you out of a tight spot. Probably the best thing to do is to establish a sporty corner and run with the theme. Take the edge off modern sporting implements by including a few well-worn, aesthetically pleasing racquets, bats or balls from times gone by. A framed print or small painting of a suitably sporting subject hung near the more modern items will also soften the blow by regaling the eye with a less brutal and far more beautiful example of the sport in question. The finished effect should feel deliberately eclectic and organic, as if today's clubs are simply joining those that have lived there for generations.

BALL SHELF A mismatched and mellow collection of old balls on a shelf interspersed with other sporting paraphernalia softens the blow of brightly coloured modern versions. There is something soft, charming but essentially masculine about this jumbled spherical display.

RACQUETS Today's fluorescent-coloured racquets can become eyesores if not handled with care. Here, their impact is softened by displaying them with a rank of older style racquets. The racquet is essentially a pleasing shape and can be celebrated if treated in this way.

GOLF CLUBS This corner of a hallway has been generously and effectively donated to golf clubs. Clubs in everyday use are propped against the wall, while fine old examples are hung in a geometric pattern. Golf balls are stored and displayed in a beaded bag.

Human beings are creatures of nature, after all, so is it any wonder that one of our most pervading characteristics is an obsession not just with our homes but with the land that surrounds them? Even the staunchest urbanite – who wouldn't know the working end of a spade let alone how to plant anything – usually has something from Mother Nature inside the home, even if it is only a vase of flowers or a few smooth pebbles to act as doorstops. Gardening, a preoccupation with nurturing the land around our homes, is a deeply embedded part of our culture and is currently enjoying a significant rise in popularity. Apart from the obvious pleasure that communing with nature brings, this popularity could also be the result of a desire to increase our personal spaces as our

outside | in

homes become steadily reduced in size, as well as a reflection of the need for an antidote to the stresses and strains of busy modern living. Interior design over the last few years has been more than keen to reflect our love of gardening. The contemporary fashion for inviting nature into the home is an elegant fusion of the traditional and the modern, superimposing popular horticultural design trends onto an evocative shared memory of happiness and security that always had roses growing around the gate and cheery vegetables arranged in serried rows in the backyard. In fact, to a large extent, when you think of the long history of floral fabrics and the historical use of trellis as an interior statement, designers have often gone into the garden for inspiration.

texture | juxtaposition

Using outdoor elements in an interior setting satisfies the rustic in all of us. On long winter evenings, reminders of summer afternoons spent in the garden can be scattered around the living room to provide a real antidote to the winter blues.

There are no limits to the range of outside objects that you can successfully bring into the home. From terracotta flowerpots and steel planters to deckchair canvas and pieces of driftwood – all are affordable ways of furnishing a room with style. Mixing outdoor finishes such as galvanized steel, rough wood and smooth pebbles with soft, conventional indoor surfaces such as wallpaper and soft rugs can make a room feel like a halfway house between the home and the garden. Informal groupings that mingle fine ceramics with roughly carved sculptural elements and growing bulbs can turn any room into a glamorous conservatory. Don't be afraid to mix and match textures: it is often the juxtaposition of different textures that helps to bring out the best in all of them. For example, in the living room pictured on the right, a miniature wooden garden bench has been used as a mantelshelf and is the perfect foil for the smooth steel fireplace below and the steel mirror above. The flower pattern and romantic lilac of the wallpaper do not upstage the more organic elements of the room but instead bring a cosy domestic comfort to the space.

DECKCHAIR FABRIC Even the most hard-cornered modernist might find this contemporary breakfast room a little unromantic now and then (above right). A panel of worn deckchair fabric in stripes of mellow colours helps to soften the ambience of the room and bring a little of the beach to family breakfasts.

DRIFTWOOD FRAME A collection of driftwood twigs has been used to make a roughly textured circular mirror frame (right). Their natural coarseness and seaside provenance set the tone for an informal arrangement of miniature boats and a naively carved lighthouse.

WOOD AND STEEL FIREPLACE This modernist steel fireplace and mirror work surprisingly well with the roughly textured wooden mantelshelf and the soft surfaces of the chair and rug (far right). There is a successful balance between hard, almost industrial finishes and the traditional prettiness of the wallpaper.

natural objects | organic displays

The pleasure we get from bringing the outside into the home is two-fold: the simple enjoyment of being close to nature's bounty, and the visual delight that a display of natural objects can create in any interior, whatever the style of decoration. Since natural objects on the whole need to be 'found' (buying driftwood from a store just isn't the same thing), a cluster of pebbles on a shelf, for example, will forever remind you of the experience you had collecting them as well as provide an attractive display for your home. As such, a natural still life will always be emotional and evocative as well as of great aesthetic value.

A grouping of natural objects looks best when it appears uncontrived. Try to imagine that a gust of wind or a gentle wave has cast the collection into your interior; if you half-close your eyes now and again when arranging the display, you will find this easy to achieve. A more formal arrangement will create a different message, almost like declaring supremacy over Mother Nature, which in a way is missing the point. An explosion of twigs cut to various lengths trying to pass itself off as an exotic flower arrangement will always fall between aesthetic stools; it is better to group the twigs as you would find them in a forest clearing so that each time you see them, you are transported instantly outside. The Oriental school of design, it is true, practises a degree of formality with natural objects but one that is counterbalanced by simplicity, allowing the eye and the mind to focus on each element in seclusion.

BASKET, VASE AND PEBBLES The textures in this arrangement of objects have a carefully considered rhythm. The rough, powdery surface of the old vase sits well with the sandy face of the unwashed pebbles, while the basket in which they rest creates a dark natural framework for the arrangement.

NATURAL STILL LIFE This urban fireplace has been made more than a little rustic by teaming found objects such as pinecones with organic elements that have been crafted into interesting shapes such as a wreath. The joy of this kind of statement is that the elements are at best free and at worst inexpensive, which means they can be changed as the mood takes you.

style lab | driftwood and pebbles

Driftwood and pebbles burrow deep into our subconscious and instantly transport us back to childhood holidays on the beach. The joy of finding, the pleasure of burrowing and the happiness at taking a natural prize home at the end of the holiday flood back. Now that we are grown-ups we can see just what pleasing shapes driftwood can achieve after years at sea, and how the elegant surface and muted colours of pebbles can animate an interior scheme.

MODERN GLASS The unexpected dissonance of finding natural objects against a contemporary glass backdrop has been fully explored here. Loft-style glass bricks make such an uncompromising urban statement that it is nice to knock the edge off their glass right angles with a little bit of nature. Against all those geometric lines, the generous curve of the fishbowl makes a restful statement.

SEASIDE THEME
For this funky
bathroom with its
porthole window
and stainless-steel
cabinet, driftwood
and pebbles in a tall
glass tank pick up on
the seaside theme
present in the mirror
and flotsam boat.
This scheme achieves
an attractive balance
between the soft
romantic face of
nature and style-led
contemporary
decorating.

ROMANTIC HEARTH Anyone who misses an open fire should try this simple arrangement of candles and pebbles on a bed of white gravel. The romantic flickering light of the candles is augmented by the wistful addition of strewn, dried rose petals. One cannot help feeling that a dinner *à deux* is about to happen ...

**GRAND
FIREPLACE**
Driftwood is so
sculptural that it can
take being camped
up a bit. Here, a
grand room with a
grand fireplace needs
a suitably grandiose
addition to the
mantelshelf, so a
contorted piece of
driftwood has been
gilded to reflect both
the candlelight and
the glow of the fire.
At the base extra-
large pebbles echo
the natural origins of
the driftwood above.

outside | in

plants | choosing

A generation ago, houseplants meant straggly spider plants scrambling over macramé pot holders, or unappetizing cheese plants sulking in a corner. Nowadays, high-maintenance houseplants have been joined by a range of more easy-come, easy-go shrubs such as lavender and rosemary. In addition, you can often use plants that are normally associated with the garden inside the home, provided they get sufficient light and are not kept in a room that is too hot.

Old-fashioned houseplants were commonly derived from unsuitable exotic stocks that required heat but little light. Like all displaced individuals culled screaming from their indigenous climates, they required a daily commitment to tender loving care and often a big dose of psychoanalysis from their owners. Although such plants are still very popular, and the natural beauty they bring into the home can be well worth the effort involved in tending them, these days simpler alternatives are just as likely to be used to plug a decorative hole – a whitewashed terracotta pot filled with lavender or rosemary, for example.

If you have a plant in your garden that you particularly like, why not pot one and bring it indoors? If the plant starts to look unhappy in its new home, simply put it back outside for a while. You will be surprised at how well some plants will grow inside – heathers seem to love spending time on an indoor windowsill and can grow exuberantly in such pampered conditions.

NATURE'S BOUNTY The variety of different plants that are readily available nowadays is staggering and, for the many people who know little about plant care, it can be difficult to choose the right one. Most garden centres and nurseries employ well-trained staff who can help you make your decision but perhaps the easiest approach from an interior design point of view is simply to buy what you like the look of. Indeed, don't even limit yourself to indoor plants or you will miss out on the wonderful outdoor variety. As long as you monitor your chosen plant's progress and ensure it has light and water, the death rate is unlikely to be too high.

plants | potting

The subject under discussion here is the pot itself. As far as the mechanics of potting are concerned, there are plenty of good gardening books and magazines that explain this procedure in depth or you could ask someone at your local garden centre for advice. Asking which potting soil would be best, what size the pot needs to be and what location would best suit the plant in question should do the trick. You can then concentrate on the enjoyable business of choosing divine containers for your plant selection.

Choosing an appropriate container is the most important aesthetic decision you have to make when displaying plants in your home. Just tapping them out of their plastic straitjacket and slipping them into something watertight and gorgeous is an instant recipe for success. Few will die, a large proportion will thrive and those that don't would probably have been subject to the laws of natural selection in any case (or so you can tell yourself).

The Victorians used to vie with each other to come up with more and more ornate china vessels for houseplants. These days, plain pots made from natural materials are often considered the most attractive, but a surprising or exotic container can transform even the most common garden bulb into a stunning centrepiece. The key is to choose a container that suits the interior, so a simple rustic earthenware pot in a country cottage-style scheme is as much a slice of plant heaven as a hyacinth in a Sèvres planter in the Salon des Glaces at Versailles.

JAPANESE PAPER VASE The sculptural qualities of this dwarf conifer have been explored to bring a feeling of topiary grandeur to a Georgian pot cupboard. The plant stays in its nursery pot, which is sleeved by a contemporary folded-paper Japanese vase. The rhythm of the complementary shapes ending in the conifer's apex is stunning.

GLAZED EARTHENWARE Spring daffodils in a cream glazed earthenware pot and saucer broadcast the end of winter in this pretty country kitchen. Even the dark green of the washing-up liquid in its heavy glass bottle picks up on the natural colour scheme.

MODERN CONTAINERS
In the loft apartment on the left, herbs have been arranged on a contemporary staircase that rises up across the wall with illuminated niches. The black plastic pots in which the plants were bought have been placed inside clear beaded plastic containers bought from a graphics supply store, though simple bubblewrap envelopes could be used to achieve a similarly stylish urban look. The rough, organic colours of the wall treatment pictured on the right are magnified through the heavy glass tank vases in which the plants are suspended over a reservoir of water.

One of the most pleasurable sights at the end a long, cold winter is the sea of colour provided by the newly emerging flowers of spring bulbs. As a flowering bulb for indoor use, hyacinths combine a heavenly scent with a bold, sculptural form that makes them a perpetually useful display staple. According to Greek legend, these pretty flowers were supposed to have sprung from Hyacinthus' blood when he was killed, or from Apollo's tears at his lover's death.

EDWARDIAN JUGS
The contrasting blues of the hyacinth flowers and the detail on the china Edwardian jugs rhyme beautifully, while the slightly incongruous addition of moss makes what might have been a rather formal statement more easy on the eye.

RHYTHMIC ROW
The bulbs, with their squiggly roots, have here been cloaked by a mantel of gravel. The simple, repetitive rhythm of the arrangement makes this mantelpiece display contemporary yet natural at the same time.

MIX-AND-MATCH CONTAINERS For this romantically modern bathroom, an informal collection of containers looks natural and uncontrived. Although each of the shapes is different, a common theme has been pursued to keep the arrangement from becoming anarchic.

GILDED URN For a bit of country house glamour, the urn has been gilded to act as a grand container for a collection of white and blue hyacinths. The unexpected joy of white hyacinths is the gorgeous fresh green they present when on the verge of flowering, which here acts as a virginal counterbalance to the richness of the gold leaf.

garden centre | form

It is not just plants that can be successfully brought into the home. Any garden centre or nursery can be raided for all manner of objects suitable for interior display. The key is to forget the proscribed function of an object and focus on its form. You may need to give some things a bit of a makeover but with very little effort it is surprising just how many outside objects can appear perfectly at home when brought inside.

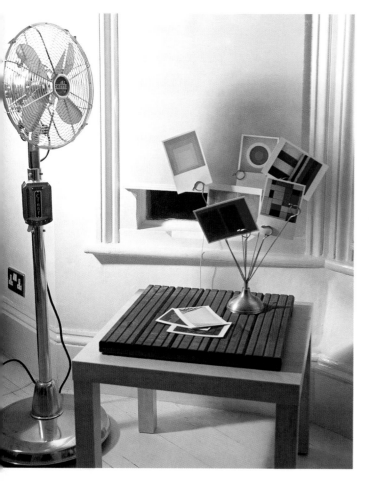

TABLETOP DECKING A panel of decking stained in a dark colour has been removed from its expected garden context and placed on this modern occasional table. The geometry of the two different elements complement each other, bringing a degree of individuality to a chain-store piece of furniture.

Interior decorators of the late 19th and early 20th centuries loved to revive the romantic and rather foolish fripperies of 18th-century rococo design. Rooms commissioned by Madame de Pompadour or Catherine the Great would undulate with beautiful cast plaster curlicues interspersed with oddly dissonant details such as rough boughs, gardening tools or twigs and trellises. Trellis – or more accurately treillage – became a real fashion trend at the beginning of the last century. Even the most exclusive hotels featured gilded ornamental trellises – a thousand miles away from the rough wooden supports for rambling roses that we would recognize but a touch of 'outside in' nevertheless.

Nowadays, it is the very roughness and woodiness of nature that we love to bring into our interiors. Conveniently, readymade trellis is not expensive and nor are sweetpea canes. Even more conveniently, homemade trellis constructed from long twigs is entirely free and can be called upon for a thousand uses.

There is also a strong pull towards the industrial in decorating at the present time. Exposed brickwork, girders and wrought-iron fire escapes have all sunk into our collective aesthetic subconscious and sit side by side with other, more gentle decorative finishes and accessories. It would be inconceivable to our grandparents that rust should have become a desirable designer finish, but thousands of pounds are spent each year by the dedicated and the style conscious on prematurely ageing metal for the interior. Nowadays, a rusty element is as romantic as a weathered terracotta pot.

SWEETPEA CANES On the right, sweetpea canes bought from a garden centre have been sprayed white, formed into a tall triangular frame and then, while the paint was still wet, sprinkled with gold leaf. It makes a surprisingly glamorous superstructure to show off a collection of costume jewellery. Above, the same structure has been moved into the living room and hung with white lights and bows to make a twinkling Christmas tree.

IVY TWIG TRELLIS Ivy
twigs, bound with raffia
and hung on a door,
create a trellis with a
series of crazy angles that
soften the sharp geometry
of the door panels.
The romantic note of the
arrangement is carried
through in the proud
display of love letters –
or at least letters from
friends who mean a lot.

GALVANIZED STEEL SHELF
This galvanized steel
shelf has been used as a
support for single freesias
in glass bottles over a
bathtub. Since the shelf
was designed for outdoor
use, it will not rust in the
bathroom. Surprisingly,
steel can be a soft,
romantic finish if placed
in the right context.

tools of the trade | multipurpose

Outdoor elements for interior use need not be solely natural – our own manmade efforts can have an unexpected beauty, too. If you look carefully and in the right way, you can find beauty in anything. Ordinary tools such as saws and gardening forks may at first appear mundane in the extreme but take them out of their context, away from their function, and just appreciate their shape, form or colour and you will discover a wealth of wonderful display objects that can be used anywhere inside the home.

It is not just the organic elements of a garden – the flowers, the plants and the pebbles – that can be brought into the home. Old gardening tools have exquisite shapes and show as much commitment to aesthetic design criteria as antique garden furniture. Interior designers latched on to this some time ago and these days glossy magazines are forever scattered with contrived interiors sprinkled with antique keys, secateurs, planes and other tools.

Like so much of contemporary living, most of us are quick to dismiss modern equivalents as lacking the same attention to detail or overall stylishness. This is often true, but not always. For many interiors, modern gardening implements can provide an amusing detail or a witty accent that proves the occupants are both in love with the great outdoors and blessed with a sense of humour. Like all things, however, you can go too far – supporting a tabletop on a pair of lawnmowers would be less of an amusing detail and more of a belly laugh. For those modern tools that really are too awful to display with pride, the simplest expedient is to blend them with more attractive older versions.

KEY AND SCISSOR BOARD Although unusable, antique keys and scissors can come in handy to take the eye away from the less attractive contemporary examples that we require for everyday use. In this context, by establishing a theme and mixing the aesthetic with the utilitarian, a successful compromise has been reached.

GARDEN FORK SHELF This witty shelf in a modern kitchen started life as a piece of MDF that has been sprayed chrome. A large hole thick enough to take the shaft of the garden fork was drilled into the bottom and the whole thing suspended on the wall with mirror plates screwed into the back of the shelf and then the wall.

SAW BLADE FRAME Old, blunt saw blades were removed from their plastic handles and the hole for the bolt that held the handle and blade together was then used to accommodate a spring bolt to join pairs of blades to form a picture frame. The bolt was then passed through a hole drilled in each corner of a piece of Perspex and on through an MDF backboard.

CHAIN RADIATOR COVER

Ugly radiators can blight lovely houses but, luckily, they can be encased in a more aesthetic way without losing their function. Here, a modern and really quite sleek solution has been used but all is not as it seems. The steel shelf is actually made from MDF and sprayed with chrome paint and the chains are inexpensive plastic ones from a DIY store, again sprayed chrome. Purists beware – real chain on this scale can be very expensive as well as extremely heavy.

The still life painters of centuries past were masters of the art of display. Their pictures were crammed with fruit, game, gorgeous vases and very often the odd architectural fragment or two. Of course, for them a 'fragment' would have been a sumptuous bust or beautifully carved urn, but even though the architectural leftovers we have access to today are usually of the house brick or garden ornament variety, they can nevertheless be used to make a soft, weather-edged statement around the home.

With just a little imagination, the bits and pieces that can be found under a layer of builder's rubble in a roadside skip can be used to create amusing, surprising and ultimately chic details within the home. Anyone who was a student in the 1970s or 1980s will remember the ubiquitous shelving units that could be made for free by stacking bricks or breeze blocks in between scaffolding planks. As an idea it still holds water today although, rather than loading the shelves with LPs, most of us would prefer to display a collection of modern glass or old books. Bricks can be put to other uses, too. Modern bricks have holes in them to keep their weight down, so try pushing candles into the holes to create a stylish candleholder.

Smaller items such as old hinges or latches can be arranged on a mantelshelf to good effect; often the fact that they are rusty is an added attraction. If you are lucky, you may find pieces of stone balustrade, stucco cornice or panels of coloured glass, which can be placed around the living room to create casual yet stylish design accents. Weathered panelled doors or shutters can be set on an appropriate base (why not try breeze blocks?) to make designer coffee tables.

SLATE TABLETOP This ordinary occasional table, bought as a flat pack from a chain store, has been given a new lease of life by arranging old roof slates on top. Bringing the natural texture of the slate into the contemporary interior creates a retro statement in keeping with the curvy swivel chair, the fur rug and the single orchid.

CHIMNEY POT CONTAINER The bare necessities of firelighting can look untidy and spider ridden. An old chimney pot begged from a builder makes a stylish vertical container for kindling. A terracotta trough filled with rosemary plants (the odd sprig thrown over the fire will perfume the room) and a colourwashed flowerpot packed with the wooden spills used for lighting the fire make use of natural objects in a stylish way.

outside | in

Now that the issues of arranging and displaying everyday possessions have been dealt with, it is time to focus on seasonal high days and holidays. In addition to the festive days recognized by faith, state or family, we all have our own special 'treat' days – spending a few moments to arrange some candles or flowers can mark a celebration as simple as 'thank goodness I've got through the week from hell' or, even better, 'I'll do it because I'm worth it'. The way an interior is decorated on festive occasions should reflect the personality of whoever is celebrating. There are many different ways to bring individual personality into an interior scheme that will set it apart from anyone else's home, and it is especially important to express this individuality when arranging

movable | feasts

objects or decorations to accompany birthdays, Christmas or other holiday festivals. Another consideration that needs to be borne in mind is how those decorations will fit into the existing style of the room. The days of Christmas decorations re-emerging every year over a lifetime are long gone, as more and more of us want our festivities to reflect changing fashions. As children, we can all remember the sudden shock of green and red that popped into our lives each Christmas. Nowadays, a green and red Christmas clashes indefensibly with lilac, marigold or cool white interiors. Festival decorating can – and should – be conceived not only to lift the spirits and set the right celebratory tone, but also to sit successfully within the existing interior design scheme.

celebrating | greetings cards

Having a huge stack of brightly printed, glossy cardboard delivered on the morning of your birthday might be emotionally touching but, all too often, finding an adequate way of integrating greetings cards into your design scheme is a complicated affair. Going for the 'grandstand look' – that is, piling the cards in serried rows on every available surface like the crowds in a sports stadium – is the obvious answer, but there are plenty of less imposing alternatives that will display the cards to best effect without completely swamping an interior.

Only the most precious and sneering aesthetes cannot bear to display their greetings cards – assuming that anyone with such an unpleasant attitude would have any friends to send them, of course. However, in the same way that you cannot choose your family, you also never get to choose your own cards. Although the vast majority of people do seem to go to great pains to send cards that are appropriate to the recipient and therefore in line with his or her design tastes, sadly, they are not always successful. The first thing you have to decide when displaying the cards is whether you are going to put all of them on show – both the good and the bad – and this is a decision only you can make. One option is to group the cards – lovely handmade cards in a prominent position, high-class art reproductions clustered together and boozy choir boys, Christmas robins and pastel-bow bedecked 'now-you-are-three' cards in a dark corner.

Greetings cards have a built-in design flaw: they are lightweight, flimsy and easily blown or knocked over. The traditional method of stringing cards in festoons was in essence a good idea, although greetings cards in swagged garlands are now considered the height of bad taste by the majority of style-conscious people. The principle, however, can be updated and used efficiently to display greetings cards in an orderly and architectural way.

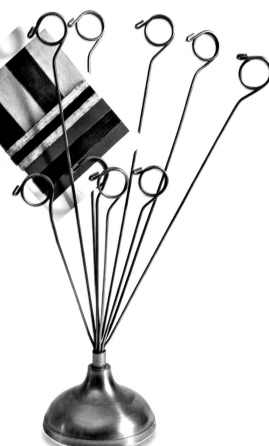

CARD TREE These sprung-wire card displays are widely available and inexpensive, and can be called upon at birthdays and other festive times of year. A series of card trees on a mantelshelf will make a festive display and, by putting your favourite cards at the front, less aesthetic designs can be consigned to the shadows.

STAIRCASE DISPLAY Brightly coloured clothespegs and a washing line make a jolly substructure on which to display children's greetings cards for an impending birthday party. Stretching the line vertically between banisters provides an ideal architectural solution, forcing the cards to become integrated with the interior rather than fight against it.

PICTURE FRAME In the picture above, the same principle as that used in the staircase display on the left has been applied within an ornate gilt frame. Gorgeous little aluminium clothespegs make a sophisticated design detail and, since the cards are pretty and non-denominational, there is no reason why they could not stay in place all year round.

movable | feasts

celebrating | gifts

There are numerous advantages to being an early bird in the present-buying stakes. Obviously, giving yourself plenty of time to consider and shop for the right gift minimizes stress enormously, but another benefit is that, provided you have wrapped the present in a suitably gorgeous manner, your gift can be incorporated into the general festive bedecking.

No matter how grown up you think you are, receiving a present in nothing more than a carrier bag is a quick recipe for a fallen crest. The object itself might be the most costly, beautiful thing you are ever likely to own, but without the drama of pulling apart lovely paper and exquisitely contrived ribbon, the experience falls flat. There is something so indulgently decadent about spending hard-earned money and precious time on creating an object whose sole purpose is to be destroyed. As we have all been taught to intone since we could first speak, 'it's the thought that counts', and the effort required in wrapping a present makes an eloquent statement of the depth of feeling that the donor of the gift holds for its recipient.

Since the wrapping of a present is ultimately doomed to a life as short as a mayfly, you can really let your hair down aesthetically. Regard gift wrapping as an opportunity to work with colours, patterns, textures or finishes that would perhaps be too strong a statement in permanent decoration. There are, of course, those who wish to celebrate through restrained understatement. Brown paper wrappings with shell-pink grosgrain bows may sound drab but, as long as there is a big statement in the scale department to offset this, a big dose of excitement is bound to be the result.

GIFT WRAPPING

There are infinite ways to wrap a present. Patterned, store-bought papers can be expensive, so do-it-yourself solutions using stationery shop purchases like stars, glitter or ordinary parcel string coloured with cold water fabric dye rely on high effort and low cost. For many of us, presents are incomplete without some form of festive bondage. The slinky act of slowly pulling a bow apart instantly puts you into a bodice-ripping frame of mind, flushed with excited anticipation.

GILDED PEBBLES If you really cannot relinquish aesthetic control and allow a gaudy celebration into your cool interior, it does not mean you have to abandon festive decoration altogether. Here, the simplicity of the ingredients – pebbles, gold leaf and lilac ribbon – makes a dignified celebratory statement that manages to maintain decorum as well as mark a special occasion. Gilding is not difficult. These pebbles were coated with spray adhesive, then sheets of fake gold leaf from an art supply shop were gently patted on.

movable | feasts

style lab | christmas trees

You could, of course, throw up your hands and resign yourself to Christmas being a taste-free zone, but there is no reason why the Christmas tree in the corner of your living room should not show the same inventive and original design solutions as the room that surrounds it.

ROMANTIC FAIRYLAND Delicate pastel-coloured organza bows of wire-edged ribbon make a floaty, transparent statement on a tree that has been lightly sprayed with glittery hairspray bought from an ordinary toiletries shop. The spray looks suitably festive and also helps to keep the tree's needles in place. Pale-hued glass beads twinkle among the branches and the whole tree has a fairyland quality that makes for a pretty, escapist display.

CONTEMPORARY CLOCKWORKS This tree has been sprayed with black hairspray from a fancy dress shop. Clock springs, with their elegant spiral shapes, make festive embellishments while clock faces provide a monochrome slant on the more traditional coloured bauble. There is no reason why the clock parts cannot form an all-year-round display in another part of the house and then be used to trim the tree at Christmas.

RICH PURPLE AND GOLD The dark green branches of this fir tree are well complemented by the baroque addition of rich purple bows arranged in a regular, formal pattern. Fake gold leaf from an art supply shop has been crumbled over the tree so that it gets caught randomly on the spiky needles. Although richly embellished, this tree stops short of being overpowering because only two decorative elements have been used.

MODERN RED AND GREEN There are plenty of people who cannot be weaned off red as their Christmas tree colour theme. Here, rather than conventional decorations in the conventional colour, red decorations have been employed from unconventional sources. Beads rather than tinsel, butterflies rather than bows and embroidered purses rather than baubles – all breathe new life into a traditional red-and-green Christmas.

For many of us, modern living seems to have lost its romance, its mystery and its glamour. Everything seems to have been measured, weighed or quantified. Electric light illuminates every corner of our lives, banishing the demons that might do us harm but at the same time forcing the fairies to flee who might otherwise have delighted us. Perhaps this is why we are all drawn to the flickering, magical illumination of candlelight.

TREE TEALIGHTS
Twinkling candles in the twilight of a midsummer garden patio create an evocative fairyland dream. Here, discarded babyfood jars with a wire loop ending in coloured beads make miniature storm shades for tealights.

Since candles serve no practical purpose in our conveniently electrically lit lives, they are difficult to justify from a practical viewpoint and therefore instantly promote themselves to the status of a luxury. Life's luxuries are what celebrating has always been about. Our great, great grandparents would be amazed to learn that we take powerful illumination so much for granted nowadays that we no longer associate it with great luxury. Even in the splendidly opulent palaces of former centuries, it was only on high days and holidays that every room was fully and expensively lit. Now when we want to celebrate an occasion, we tend to go the other way and use primitive candlelight to mark our indulgent mood. Of course, the reason for this could well be that at the back of our minds lies a childish delight in remembering the moment our fully lit, candle-bedecked birthday cake was brought from the kitchen into a hushed and darkened childhood party.

SALVAGED CANDLESTICKS Rough wooden blocks drilled with holes big enough to take a candle make a simple, almost Shaker-style statement in a fireplace. For anyone who has a non-working fireplace, remember that clustered candles on the hearth make a plausible alternative to a roaring fire and generate both flickering light and, believe it or not, a degree of warmth.

CANDLELIGHT TREAT

We all have moments when we know we have more than earned this type of candlelight treat. A long, hot bath surrounded by lit tealights, with bruised lavender leaves gently releasing their fragrance into the water as floating candles bob serenely across its surface, form the perfect invitation to enter the warm watery depths of hedonistic pleasure. Once you are installed – make sure you blow out the floating candles before getting into the tub – you will be on another planet, a gentler, kinder, more romantic place, for at least as long as the water stays warm.

candles | embellishing

Since candles are so crucial to our celebrations, spending some time making them look as opulent and indulgent as the light they throw out seems more than justifiable. These days the candle maker's art is achieving new and dizzying heights of creativity, thanks to the current healthy market their wares enjoy. Art candles, however, come at a price but luckily, with a little imagination, there are a thousand and one ways in which you can produce similar results yourself.

When doing the job for which it was designed — gently gilding the objects in a darkened room with soft and romantic apricot light — the candle reigns supreme. All too often, however, in the cold light of day the guttered, untidy mass of wax left over from the previous night's romantic drinks *à deux* fails to lift the spirits. In the past, when candles were an essential fact of life and the household's only means of banishing the dark, it was considered the height of slovenliness to leave candles in their sticks during the daytime. Real wax candles were very expensive and had to be strictly rationed. For many servants, part of their daily salary was the remnants of their master's candles left over at dawn, which could then be recycled for the servants' own private use.

Even though candles play such a precious part in reviving our flagging spirits and rekindling our faith in romance at night, during the day they should, like all other elements in a design scheme, pay their aesthetic way. However appealing their price tag, cheap candles are cheap for a reason. They simply will not burn as well or for as long as those that cost a little more. Tempting though it may be to buy a thousand tealights for the same cost as a single lightbulb, they will burn out much, much faster than better quality candles.

BEADED COLUMN CANDLES
The thick candles pictured above rarely burn right down. They are designed to hollow out, leaving an illuminated core that shines through the translucent outer tube of wax. That's the theory, anyway. On the left, glass beads have been threaded onto dressmaking pins and pushed into the candle through the holes in the middle of sequins. On the right, jet tube beads have been attached to the candle by pushing the pin through the centre and then forcing the bead into the wax at varying depths.

GOTHIC CANDLES The rivulets of solidified wax that festoon guttered candles can be utilized to make a baroquely decadent statement in the right kind of interior. These candles are romantic in a Byronic, Gothic-novel sort of way and the spikily elegant shapes of the brass clock hands echo the jagged edges of the candles to which they have been pinned. At night they reflect the light as a golden shape (above), while by day their good-natured glitter makes the craggy group of candles more light-hearted (right).

BEADED TEALIGHTS Fine wire and coloured glass beads have been used to make glamorous little nests for a pair of tealights (left). The flexibility of the wire allows the nests to be bent around curved shapes such as the rolled lip of a bathtub. For extra stability, twisted wire arms reach down and firmly clasp the underside of the lip.

EVOCATIVE CANDLELIGHT

Even in the most considered, stylish, successful interiors, you need to introduce a random factor every now and then to breathe new life into the scheme. Lighting changes the mood of any room instantly, and the soft-focus ambience created by candlelight is both powerful and evocative. Everything looks better with the lights out and the candles lit. More importantly, life feels better with the lights out and the candles lit, which is why candlelight plays such a huge role in helping us to celebrate – it cheers us up and smooths out the bumpy bits. Here, small cubes of a lightweight wood have been screwed at regular intervals onto an MDF backboard, then the whole structure painted midnight blue. When set against this kind of framework, even tiny tealights can achieve a dramatic impact.

flowers | arranging

After candles, the next thing on our celebratory shopping list is flowers. Unlike candles, however, flowers have always been regarded as a luxury rather than a necessity – tulip bulbs were once prized as highly as gold – although, during various periods in history, flowers have served more functions than simply to delight the nose and the eye.

OPULENT TABLE CENTRE The traditional furniture and rich greens of this dining room (left) call for a sculptural, deep-coloured arrangement of flowers to set the tone for a celebratory dinner party. The Oriental note established by the window shutters has inspired a casual allusion to Eastern arranging with the contorted willow and blue-glazed, Oriental-inspired vase.

OUTDOOR LUNCH The hard lines of the modern dining table (far right) have been softened by an organza runner, which instantly lightens the mood. Early summer flowers in pastel colours have been informally arranged in an aluminium vase that alludes aesthetically to the garden. The effect is informal, fun and breezy, with herbs squeezed into the arrangement for extra scent.

Before the advent of giant refrigerated flower trucks that ferry flowers around the world regardless of season, you could tell exactly where you were in the year by looking at a flower arrangement. The whites and yellows of spring bulbs enlivened by fresh green hellebores gave way to pastel blossom arrangements as spring slid into summer. The purple-blues and various pinks of the early summer months would be replaced by hotter oranges and reds at the end of the season. By the autumn, colour came from foliage or late roses and, of course, by midwinter the slick green of holly with its inevitably red berry was all that was available.

Now the seasons overlap as never before and exotic newcomers have been coaxed into the florist's shop. Flowers are a labour-intensive form of decorating and ultimately, of course, short-lived. Like all festive embellishments, flowers do not last beyond the period they have been contrived to celebrate and so we are, thankfully, not given the opportunity to tire of them. Although there has been an overwhelming movement towards simplicity in floral arrangement in recent years – the restrained decorum of a glass tank full of white tulips is, in the right context, to die for – for more boisterous feasts there is no reason why you cannot opt for something a little more chaotic, brimming with different colours and scents. Even when the flowers have died, the flower heads can be dried as an emotional and aesthetic reminder of the arrangement they came from and, therefore, the event they celebrated.

DRIED FLOWERS The bleak winter months can be enlivened florally with a shallow bowl filled with the dried heads from a summer bouquet (left), providing a touching but nevertheless beautiful reminder of things past. The scent from the politely decaying blooms can be enhanced and prolonged by adding a few drops of perfumed oil every now and again.

CHIC SIMPLICITY In the picture on the right, the celebration could be anything – Happy Wednesday, Thanks for helping me change the wheel on the car or Happy Mother's Day. The fact that the glass tank of white tulips has been placed, rather unusually, on a chair shows how special the thought behind the arrangement is – the flowers have been moved as close to the bed as possible in order to delight the lucky recipient immediately on awakening. It is a natural, informal look that is worth the effort involved in contriving to look uncontrived.

flowers | containers

If you read women's magazines from the 1950s, you will discover article after fascinating article about the importance of having a sufficient quantity of the right kind of vase. The truth these days, however, is that although we might have one or two attractive vases, if we are in the mood to celebrate, the number of flower arrangements could easily outnumber the designated containers.

Imagine a gorgeous, rich, dense bouquet of flowers in a gorgeous, rich, densely embellished vase – but what does this really amount to? Answer: a large, overblown lump of not-quite-art. As is so often the case, getting display right means understanding the relationships between objects in order to achieve the right balance. Of course, the Victorians believed that pattern and colour should be crammed into every corner and onto every available surface. Today, we like a cooler, more balanced approach to display that often means either underplaying the container of a rich bouquet or underplaying the arrangement in an ornate vase. As a result, suitable receptacles for flowers can come from the most unlikely sources. Milk bottles, old fishbowls, jam jars and plastic pen tidies – they can all work if the flowers are fresh and jaunty enough to delight the eye. Playing down the vase element in a festive floral arrangement can be a highly effective way of making celebratory flower displays coordinate more closely with today's more informal interiors.

PLASTIC PEN TIDY It is somebody's birthday at the office and there are no vases around, so what do you do? In the picture above, a plastic pen tidy has been commandeered along with some antique inkwells to hold simple birthday posies.

FESTIVE WELCOME

A variety of vessels has been pressed into service to make a celebratory statement on this front doorstep. Fishbowls and flowerpots mingled with vases and candles in glasses will make the arriving guests confident that they have not only found the right party but that they will be truly welcome within.

GLASS BOTTLES

The serene and simple space of the kitchen pictured far left would be overpowered by an overblown flower arrangement in a grand vase, so two clouded-glass bottles have been chosen instead. They provide the ideal transparent green to tone with the grey-green foliage and dusty purple flower heads of the sea holly.

feasts | setting the mood

The festive table need not rely solely on flowers and candles for its impact. Coloured fabrics, ripened fruit and even the choice of china can all be used to set the right tone and mood. In the same way that we like to dress ourselves up for a celebration, dressing up a room will instantly conjure the party spirit.

Just two hundred years ago, rooms specifically designated as dining rooms were rare. On a whim, the master or mistress of the household would decide which room offered the right atmosphere, mood or view for any particular dining occasion. Sometimes the party would be accommodated somewhere in the grounds. Nowadays, most of us restrain ourselves to plastic cups and easily stacked furniture for outdoor entertaining, but our forebears would have had the table formally set, the linen perfectly pressed and a full set of silver and crystal sparkling in the sunlight.

There is something lovely about seeing a grand, formal party arrangement in the informal context of the garden but today, of course, we cannot rely on servants to do all the hard work involved. Remember, though, that preparing for a celebration can be half the fun. After all, going about decorating for a party while preoccupied with how long the whole thing will take to clear up is a rather grudging attitude. Why bother giving the celebration at all? Once again, the obvious effort expended on achieving the right effect surely expresses the depth of the emotion.

DINING À DEUX A private shared moment is about to be celebrated here. The context for the celebration has been carefully chosen and, to heighten the exceptional experience, the table settings have been laid on an embroidered throw on the floor. Elements with a rich colour theme in common have been gathered from around the house to make a one-off, special, luxuriously Eastern party scheme.

CHIMPS TEA PARTY A birthday celebration for children need not be a riot of clashing colours and objects. The table setting on the right features primary colours in the tablecloth, cups and food that make a boisterous statement, while the plain white china has been upgraded with oven-fixed porcelain paint. Merit stars strewn over the table could be used to bribe good behaviour from the small celebrants.

INTERIOR AL FRESCO A picnic atmosphere pervades the table arrangement pictured below left on the opposite page, as rustic salads and coarsely cut slices of bread serve both to decorate the table and to hint at the simple but hearty feast to follow. The wire and coloured-bead collars made for the primary coloured candles provide a note of simplified glamour, and a garden container full of fresh spring flowers brings the outside into the interior.

RUSTIC CELEBRATION Despite the sophisticated context of the room on the left, a celebratory lunch has been given a simplistic, almost rural feel by the use of Cornish ware jugs and rough linen runners laid across the table. Mismatched oak chairs continue the informal mood.

METROPOLITAN DELIGHT In the table setting below, plain china has been upgraded into party mode with a scarlet runner and matching napkins made from fabric remnants. Rather than sewing the hems of the fabric, iron-on hemming tape was used to turn the edges.

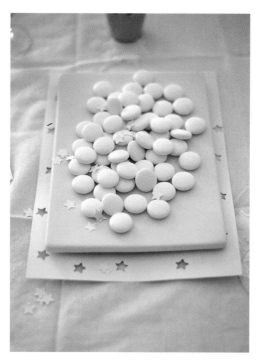

ROMANTIC FEAST The all-white table has been given special prominence in the room by the installation of an impromptu muslin canopy. Fairy lights, white linen and the simplicity of white tulips create a fresh and innocent confection of a table setting. A star-shaped hole punch was used not only to make pretty perforated paper tablemats and place-setting labels but also to produce quantities of white paper stars with which to strew the table. A single white tulip laid over each of the plates is a beautiful finishing touch with which to welcome guests.

sourcing products

Finding the right decorative element to plug a gap, balance a colour scheme or improve a composition really just boils down to keeping an open mind. Remember that everyday items can be equally efficient in interior terms as the most expensive *objets d'art* from upmarket antiques shops. Junk shops and car boot sales are fertile sources of products, and don't ignore the stored detritus that we all have in the attic, garage or garden shed.

DIY stores these days are packed emporia of decorative potential. However, you may find some of the most efficient makeover items not with the vases or photograph frames but instead hiding in the more gritty corners of the shop. Even the most extraordinary and unlikely bits of plumbing kit such as plastic U-bends or lengths of pipe can be turned into exotically industrial vases or plinths for houseplants. Never forget that anything can be given a makeover; finding the right shape or form is worth its weight in gold.

Art supply shops and craft stores are also worth regular culling, not just for the kinds of materials we are accustomed to using for makeover projects but also for raw materials that can be utilized directly in displays. Hoop embroidery frames designed to stretch fabric can be sneakily sidestepped into functioning as photograph or picture frames. Ceramic palettes with their shallow dishes make a good framework in which to display small collections of items.

Roadside skips act as magnets for foragers. A broken old architrave could easily provide a suitable length of timber to edge a shelf after the damaged ends have been cut away. Old-fashioned doorknobs patinated by years of use are mellow, tactile forms in their own right. Old bricks, once they have been stripped of their build-up of concrete, can become simple plinths for objects on a mantelshelf or pleasingly rustic candleholders.

The most valuable resource, however, is imagination. The raw materials are out there, surrounding us, but because we see them every day they take on a cloak of invisibility. In fact, you will probably find that it is when you are wandering aimlessly that the world's most successful display solution will jump off a shelf, out of a skip or down from a loft to greet you.

some useful addresses

UNITED KINGDOM

DIY stores:
B & Q
Portswood House
1 Hampshire Corporate
   Park
Chandlers Ford
Hampshire SO53 3YX
tel: 02380 256 256
www.diy.com

Homebase
Beddington House
Railway Approach
Wallington
Surrey SM6 0HB
tel: 020 8784 7200
www.homebase.co.uk

Craft supplies:
Fred Aldous Ltd
37 Lever Street
Manchester M60 1UX
tel: 0161 236 2477

Candles:
Prices
110 York Road
London SW11 3RU
tel: 020 7228 2001

Pictures and frames:
Picture Warehouse
Abbey Road Motor Centre
Belsize Road
London NW6 4AB
tel: 020 7328 6915

Lighting:
Christopher Wray
591–593 Kings Road
London SW6 2YW
tel: 020 7736 8434
www.christopherwray.com

Storage:
The Holding Company
Burlington House
184 New Kings Road
London SW6 4NF
tel: 020 7610 9160
*www.theholdingcompany.
   co.uk*

Shelfstore
6/8 Frognal Parade
158 Finchley Road
London NW3 5HH
tel: 020 7794 0313

**Furniture and home
accessories:**
Aero
96 Westbourne Road
London W2 5RT
tel: 020 7221 1950

The Conran Shop
Michelin House
81 Fulham Road
London SW3 6RD
tel: 020 7589 7401
www.conran.co.uk

Habitat
196 Tottenham Court
   Road
London W1P 9LD
tel: 020 7255 2545
www.habitat.co.uk

Ocean Home Shopping
Freepost Lon 811
London SW8 4BR
tel: 0870 848 4840

Garden accessories:
The English Garden
   Collection
tel: 0870 606 0304

UNITED STATES

Craft supplies:
Amsterdam Art
1013 University Avenue
Berkeley, CA 94710
tel: 415 548 9663

Sam Flax
111 8th Avenue
New York, NY 10011
tel: 212 620 3060

Sax Arts & Crafts
PO Box 51700
New Berlin, WI 53151
tel: 414 784 6880

Pictures and accessories:
Design Ideas
PO Box 2967
Springfield, IL 62708
tel: 217 753 3081

Kate's Paperie
561 Broadway
New York, NY 10012
tel: 212 941 9816

Lighting:
Sirmos
979 Third Avenue
New York, NY 10022
tel: 718 786 5920

Storage:
The Container Store
2000 Valwood Parkway
Dallas, TX 75234
tel: 800 733 3532

Hold Everything
PO Box 7807
San Fransicso, CA 94120
tel: 800 421 2264

**Furniture and home
accessories:**
Aero
132 Spring Street
New York, NY 10012
tel: 212 966 1500

Bed, Bath & Beyond
620 Avenue of the
   Americas
New York, NY 10011
tel: 212 255 3550

The Bombay Company
tel: 800 829 7789

Coconut Company
131 Greene Street
New York, NY 10012
tel: 212 559 1940

Ikea
tel: 800 434 4532

Inside Out
11 Railroad Avenue
East Hampton, NY 11937
tel: 516 329 3600

Laura Ashley
tel: 800 367 2000

Pier One
461 Fifth Avenue
New York, NY 10017
tel: 212 447 1610
www.pier1.com

Garden accessories:
Smith & Hawken
Two Arbor Lane
Box 6900
Florence
KY 41022 6900
tel: 800 776 3336

index

A

animals, beds for 86–7
architectural details, emphasizing 24
architectural fragments 124–5
artwork display 72, 73
asymmetry 15, 20–3, 33, 34–5

B

bath, tealights in 138–9
bookshelves, colour-coded 38–9
button collection 60–1

C

candles:
  embellishing 140–1
  to create ambience 136–9
candlesticks 43
celebrations 126–7
chandeliers 26–7
  adding crystal drops to 46–7
  in front of window 25
children:
  artwork display 72, 73
  birthday table setting 152
  collections 73
  storage out of reach of 72–7
  toy storage 70–1
chimney breast, as feature wall
  56–7
chimney pots, as containers 125
china and earthenware:
  displaying out of reach 74–5
  grouping by colour 36–7
  grouping by pattern 66–7
Christmas 127
Christmas trees, style lab 134–5
clothes, as decoration 82–5
clutter 6, 68–9
coats, storing 80
collections:
  children's 73
  of small objects 58–61
colour:
  maximizing 49
  single, arrangements in 36–7
computers 90

containers:
  for flowers 148–9
  for plants 108–11
context 46–7, 51
Le Corbusier 20
crystal:
  bowl, playing down 28
  drops, adding to chandelier 46
cutlery, silver 28
cutlery tray, as frame 58

D

dado rails, height 52
daylight, maximizing 49
deckchair fabric 98
dimensions, adjusting 50–1
dolls 59
doll's house furniture 56
doorstep, flower arrangements on 149
downscaling 40–1
driftwood 98–9
  style lab 102–5

E

earthenware *see* china and
  earthenware
electronic equipment 90–1
emphasis 24

F

family home 68–93
feasts, setting the mood 150–5
feature walls 56–7
fireplaces 16
  candles in 104, 137
  on feature wall 56–7
  found objects in 100, 104
  gilded arrangements on 44–5, 105
  increasing visual size 52–3
  mirror over 48
  steel 98
  style lab 30–3
fish tanks 88–9
flowers:
  arrangements 144–7
  containers for 148–9
  dried 146
formal 14–15

found objects 100–1
frames:
  architectural:
    embellishing 56–7
    enhancing 52–5
  asymmetrical arrangements 20
  cutlery tray as 58
  displaying cards in 129
  for photographs 78–9
  for postcards 64–5
  of saw blades 121
  silver 28–9, 30
  symmetrical arrangements 17
  for TV 92
furniture, reducing apparent size
  50–1

G

garden objects:
  indoors 116–19
  tools as decoration 120–1
garnitures 73
gift wrapping 130–1
gold leaf 26
greetings cards 128–9

H

handbags, as decoration 82–3
height, increasing 48
human body, symmetry 15, 16

I

informal 14–15

K

key board 120
kitchen shelves 34

L

lamps, standard, reducing proportions
  50
lampshades:
  buttons on 60–1
  photographs on 63